Achieving Accountability in Business and Government

Achieving Accountability in Business and Government

Managing for Efficiency, Effectiveness, and Economy

D. R. SHELDON

Q

QUORUM BOOKS
Westport, Connecticut • London

Library of Congress Cataloging-in-Publication Data

Sheldon, D. R. (Debra R.)
  Achieving accountability in business and government : managing for
efficiency, effectiveness, and economy / D. R. Sheldon.
      p.   cm.
  Includes bibliographical references and index.
  ISBN 0–89930–759–0 (alk. paper)
  1. Auditing, Internal. 2. Management audit. 3. Administrative
agencies—Auditing. 4. Administrative agencies—Management.
  I. Title.
  HF5668.25.S5   1996
  657'.458—dc20   95–808

British Library Cataloguing in Publication Data is available.

Library of Congress Catalog Card Number: 95–808
ISBN: 0–89930–759–0

First published in 1996

Quorum Books, 88 Post Road West, Westport, CT 06881
An imprint of Greenwood Publishing Group, Inc.

Printed in the United States of America

The paper used in this book complies with the
Permanent Paper Standard issued by the National
Information Standards Organization (Z39.48–1984).

10 9 8 7 6 5 4 3 2 1

Contents

Figures

Preface

How frequently we hear expressions of amazement at the absence of accountability. Everywhere we turn, whether the administration of the federal government, bureaucracy at the state and local level, corporate management, university administrations, or local retailers, the refrain is repeated: "What are these people *doing*?" People decry fast food restaurants that are not fast, teachers who can't teach, administrators who can't manage, governments who spend tax dollars callously; the list seems almost limitless. Frustrated, citizens balk at approving needed tax increases, and private shareholders whose interests have been slighted for management gains turn away from traditional capital markets. International trade barriers are erected by mistrusting union members. And thus, the dysfunctional cycle intensifies. Negativism and increasing isolationism work against effective solutions.

This book examines the accountability crisis, and proposes solutions. The particular focus is on a technique that has worked exceedingly well for many organizations: comprehensive or "value for money" auditing. Audits of this nature zero in on the elements of economy, efficiency, and effectiveness, and use performance measures to evaluate an organization's progress toward carefully deliberated goals.

In this decade and in previous ones, managements have been exhorted to use other techniques: zero-based budgeting, re-engineering, bottom-up management and total quality management have been touted as cure-alls. These techniques and others are not mutually exclusive and can integrate well with the use of value-for-money auditing and enhance its effects.

As economies of developed nations slow down, as populations grow and resources become ever more constrained, as redistribution of resources strain nations' abilities to adapt to the needs of different constituencies, value-for-money auditing offers cogent ways to meet the many challenges before us. This book is written for citizen groups, for managers, for government officials, and for students of management who will be leading us into making the twenty-first century more responsive than the last.

Chapter 1

Introduction:
The Mandate for Accountability

INTRODUCTION

Whether transnational or domestic, corporations and government seem to be mired in a crisis of accountability. This crisis includes diseases of inefficiency, lack of competitiveness, moral and ethical lapses, and intentional fraud for self-gain. Ineffectiveness, deficiencies in quality, the demise of teamwork, short-sightedness, waste, and labor inequity are topics creeping into even the most casual of business luncheons. The absence of accountability at all levels of organizations is endemic in the workplace today. This book targets managers who want to achieve accountability: those who want to understand what it is, why it's important, how to measure it, how to implement it, and how to know when the system is working and when it's not. It explores the technique of performance auditing, including a state-of-the-art synopsis of current concepts, unresolved issues, and potential functions of performance audit. Managers and auditors alike will find a relevant overview for practitioners in both the public and the private sector. Internal auditors will find it particularly relevant. In addition, it takes a managerial approach for use by executives and operating officers concerned with controlling and directing the operations of their business units. Performance auditing is widely used for managerial evaluation of economy, effectiveness, and efficiency. It relies upon the implementation of a competent system of internal control, and therefore the internal auditor plays an essential role in the performance audit process. Furthermore, because of the comprehensive nature of the performance audit, many subject area specialists are required at all levels of management. The communication of the results of the performance audit, and recommendations for control improvements are often coordinated through external auditors to the internal audit office, and the audit committee of the board of directors. In the federal government, the use of inspector generals and chief financial officers offers broad new opportunities for the achievement of accountability. In state, local, and municipal governments, performance audits offer mechanisms to evaluate how to do more with less, even in a polarized and politically charged community. Society is infused with people asking for more, and willing (or only able) to pay less. In the private sector, better accountability and enhanced information on management effectiveness fosters a more efficient capital market. In this environment of decreased resources and increased need, performance auditing is a pivotal tool in making resource allocation decisions.

WHAT IS THE CRISIS OF ACCOUNTABILITY?

The Public Sector

Mismanagement costs billions of dollars. Victims may be as diverse as the population itself: shareholders, taxpayers, university students, library users, and managers themselves. Consider, for example, the recently released report of the U.S. House of Representatives Government Operations Committee, "Managing the Federal Government: A Decade of Decline."[1] Overall, it is alleged that *$300 billion* has been wasted since 1988. Programs appear to have lost sight of their objectives and wasted tax dollars mount up. The staff report is particularly critical of faulty internal controls in federal agencies, and ineffective reporting systems. For example,

- the Bureau of Indian Affairs manages $2,100,000,000 in trust funds. The financial records are so inadequate that the Tribal and Indian accounts are largely unsupervised.

- amid criticism of Department of Energy contracting, its inspector general put in motion corrective action that included auditing major contractors on a five-year basis. After five years, a dismal record of 348 audits had been accomplished out of a needed 2,500.

- one group of farmers couldn't win. While the Department of Agriculture was paying them $379,000,000 *not* to grow crops, the Department of Interior was granting them subsidies for irrigation for the production of cotton, corn, barley, and rice.

- Pentagon warehouses contain $21,000,000,000 worth of unnecessary and surplus spare parts, and over $9,000,000,000 in unnecessary materials.

Representative John Conyers has been particularly interested in reducing federal waste and mismanagement, suggesting a wide-spread plan of oversight. He joins the many inspector generals, chief financial officers, Grace Commission participants of the Reagan era, and General Accounting Office auditors who want to "reinvent government." Congress, the source of many hearings on the abysmal record of federal loan programs, health care benefit programs, defense procurement, timberland management, and Superfund toxic waste removal funds, amid others, admits to culpability for cutting back on audits as they cut back on other funding.

The Environmental Protection Agency has been particularly singled out for mismanagement. A scathing review by the Center for Resource Economics notes that EPA throws its resources at the wrong problems. The agency uses only 7 percent of its budget to attack pesticides and air pollution which are our most significant sources of health and ecological problems, reserving more than 50 percent of its funds to monitor effluent from industry and on the removal of inactive toxic waste.[2]

Improper supervision, inaccurate reporting, and questionable personal ethics continue to make headlines. A study on NASA found that 43 percent of night shift employees were asleep, literally, on the job. Employees at other agencies helped themselves at taxpayer expense to such items as a wine press, an expensive grandfather clock, and precious coins.[3] The Dayton Daily News and Cox News Service researched waste and fraud and found extensive abuse of disability compensation; television networks tracked "disabled" individuals who were drawing up to 75 percent of their former salaries, and photographed them in intensive leisure and athletic activities. In all, the General Accounting Office has issued over fifteen major reports to Congress, complaining that mandated controls have not been enacted, that waste and fraud continue, and that mandated audits fail to occur. "Research and tell" books on federal mismanagement continue to draw substantial audiences. Two very recent ones document the inability of the bureaucracy to use common sense.[4] For example, in coal-rich parts of Europe, American military bases must use coal shipped from the U.S. mainland for fuel.

The Private Sector

This mismanagement is not limited to our federal government. Consider here the example of the new European Bank for Reconstruction and Development. This bank was created in large part to provide funding for infrastructure development in Eastern Europe and to foster a capitalistic economy in the region. The Bank's head has thus far spent $300,000,000 for administrative expenses including nine bank dining rooms and rare marble facing in the lobby, and has only lent out a total of $240,000,000. Administrative expenses also include nearly $1 million for private planes for the Bank's head, who refuses to take commercial air flights.

Or consider some positive news. In one two-inch obituary in the *Washington Post,* the death of a Blue Cross and Blue Shield official is noted. More than half of the obituary is devoted to noting that the deceased reduced the organization's overhead from 11 percent to 5 percent, and achieved material savings from more closely managed reimbursement practices. Clearly someone saw these events as the crowning achievement of the life of the deceased!

Professionals in Crisis

Professionals are increasingly besieged by accusations of incompetence, fraud, waste, and unethical behavior as well. Doctors, lawyers, accountants, and engineers are regularly showcased in the media for overcharging, inadequate diligence, ethical lapses, and failing to protect innocent parties. Recording artist Billy Joel has gone to court to recoup $90 million from his attorneys. He has accused them of failing to tell him of a conflict of interest involving CBS, other attorneys, and one of his previous managers. Joel's current attorneys on the case have articulated that they wish to curtail unsavory practices in the entertainment field.[5] Accountants have been particularly denounced for alleged failures, and have frequently been the "deep pockets" into which aggrieved parties have reached. Lawsuits against accountants have resulted in litigants' attempts to recover financial sums far in excess of accountants' fees. The profession, concerned about both public image as well as a misunderstanding of their audit function, have responded. In 1992, the Committee of Sponsoring Organizations (COSO) of the Treadway Commission issued a rather significant report: *Internal Control—Internal Framework*. This particular Committee represented a very broad representation of the business world, including law makers, directors, regulators, attorneys, business operating officers, and others. Thinking that their work was done, they waited for the report to be integrated into practice. However, controversy ensued. An assistant comptroller general at the General Accounting Office attacked the report as a "retreat from the public interest."[6] In effect, the GAO is of the opinion that reporting of internal controls under the COSO report does not go far enough toward making the public aware of achievement of controls. The series of audits described in this book, including compliance audits, operational audits, attest audits, and performance audits are some of the formalized reports that GAO would like to see included in financial reports. In a letter of October 30, 1992, a GAO official noted his assertion that the COSO requirements were inadequate to demonstrate a renewed interest in improved corporate management and oversight.

In fact, while business fraud is infinitesimally minor when one considers the size of overall business revenues, the frauds that exist receive widespread publicity and erode public confidence. Sloans Supermarkets were indicted in New York for purchasing grocery store coupons obtained from newspapers and then submitting them to manufacturers as if the coupons were the result of consumer purchases. The president and CEO as well as other officers are accused of laundering money and mail fraud.[7] In another case, MiniScribe debt holders received $550 million in a suit against the accountants and investment bankers of the firm. The company chairman was indicted for issuing inaccurate financial statements, which included taking income when no sales occurred, overstating inventory, and reporting unrealistic rates of growth.[8] The premiere fashion design house of Chanel has experienced problems as well. In an ironic twist, two men whom Chanel employed to investigate fraud and to seize copied Chanel merchandise, perpetrated their own fraud, including submitting bills for goods they sold which they had obtained from unauthorized sellers. The case includes several New York City " blues," who stand accused of selling fake Chanels which were stored as evidence in another case.[9] In the international arena, recent cases have included a massive Reserve Bank of India securities fraud. In Japan, Kanemaru resigned from Parliament amid acknowledgment that he both accepted payoffs and failed to pay personal taxes he owed.

WHAT DOES ACCOUNTABILITY MEAN?

In effect, the crisis of accountability includes mismanagement: real, imagined, intentional, or inadvertent. The solutions to accountability include formal, public reports from which interested parties can glean such information as performance, potential for performance, compliance with laws and regulations, security for employees, and other relevant information. Timely and accurate information provides a stable backdrop from which the public is able to discern management effectiveness. Interested parties may be shareholders, employees, lawmakers, regulators, debt holders, potential investors, or communities where the organization is located. V/hen adequate, timely, and relevant information is achieved, accountability problems will decline, and perceptions of management will better correspond with actual management performance.

Performance Auditing and Its Role in Achieving Accountability

The model of performance measurement includes evaluation of *efficiency*, *effectiveness*, and *economy*. Extensions of the model relate these performance measures to *relevance* and *sustainability*. Reporting the results of a review of these factors provides the public with the information needed to make allocation decisions.

Performance audit utilizes three critical factors for effective management as a focus: *economy, efficiency, and effectiveness. Economy* refers to the utilization of resources, whether these resources are tangible, such as current or fixed assets, or intangible resources, which are not "booked" on financial statements, such as human resources inside the organization. Economy is achieved by having obtained these resources at the lowest possible cost. For example, if the state of California contracts to repair buckled highways due to an earthquake, it should do so at the lowest possible cost. A bidding system would ensure that this objective was attained; clearly, the request for bids would have to be written such that the specifications are exact and preclude underbidding due to sacrificing quality for cost. However, economy alone will not achieve the best possible outcome of the highway project. A bid may be economical in the sense that it represents least cost, while not achieving the objective of efficiency. Following the logic of the buckled highway, the highway may be put back in working order by hauling away the rubble, rebuilding badly damaged sections, and putting another coat of asphalt on the rest of the roadway. This policy, done at the least cost due to the bidding process, will enable citizens to return rapidly to the clogged highways which they experienced prior to the disruption of the earthquake. This policy may not, however, be *efficient*. The use of the term "*efficient*" in the performance audit context refers to attaining the best possible use of scarce resources, or sometimes, the best possible "mix" of resources to get the job done. The state highway commission has some currently owned assets to build, maintain, and repair highways. These include both tangible assets, such as trucks, gravel, and barricades, as well as direct (workmen) and indirect (managerial and supervisory) labor. The state will need to redirect the efforts of the highway commission to defer their building and maintenance functions in favor of allocating all available resources to the emergency repair function. This is to say that while the bid from the outside contractor was economical in responding to a minimum bid, it is not efficient if the job could be done quicker by supplementing the contractor's work with state highway crews which were previously allocated to building new roads. This means that an objective function has been changed to make repairing existing roads a higher priority than building new ones. The mix of services has been reconfigured within the highway office and the repair function is pulling in resources from the public and private sector. We now have obtained the best and fastest rebuilding of buckled highways at the least cost, permitting citizens to resume their arduous commutes as soon as possible.

But we may not have achieved the best outcome. We have not yet considered the third "e," the concept of *effectiveness*. Have we achieved our public policy objectives? Why did we build the highways in the first place? Were they built prior to the initiation of the extensive and modern mass transit system, BART (Bay Area Rapid Transit)? Are the old highways discouraging use of rapid transit, thereby increasing the costs of running BART due to a lower volume? Has this further depressed mass transit use because the car is more economical or convenient to the individual? If we used some of the old highway bed to provide suburban parking for citizens commuting into the city, would that make the BART system more economical as well as more convenient? It may also allow citizens to commute into the urban area more quickly, and reduce the primary form of air pollution in the city: automobile exhaust fumes. What other alternatives exist to compete with the decision to rebuild the same highway in the same place as it was prior to the disruption of an earthquake?

These questions are the dilemma of effectiveness. The effectiveness dimension refers to selecting the best alternative method of achieving management's objectives; in this case, we want to bring people cheaply, quickly, and conveniently into the urban area, while maintaining air quality. And rebuilding the existing highways, albeit at the least cost, and using the least amount of scarce resources, may not be effective. Rather, seizing the opportunity afforded by the tragedy of an earthquake may permit the government to better serve its constituents in the long run. For "effectiveness," rebuilding the old highway does not fill the bill; rather, that decision perpetuates bad traffic, poor air quality, and long and expensive commuting. The effectiveness dimension would delve into considering alternatives to building the highway which might better serve the Bay area citizens.

The concept of *relevance* evaluates the relationship between the outputs achieved, and their influence on program goals. In the largest sense, the question is, "Have the expenditures improved transportation for citizens in the Bay area?" Furthermore, how much have they improved it, and in what ways. We may explore, for example, commuting times, environmental concerns, use of scarce resources such as fossil fuels, convenience for citizens, etc.

Sustainability is a factor in performance audit in gauging the effects of the outcomes over time. For example, how durable are the outcomes? Will we have to build a new system in five years or ten? Have we evaluated changing technology which will affect the transportation system? Are population growth, economic growth, shifting populations from urban to suburban areas considered? Explicit evaluations of durability or sustainability factors lead managers toward solutions of accountability over time.

OVERVIEW OF THE BOOK

In the first section, the benefits of performance audit are explored. The environment in which accountability has been problematic is reviewed. The discussion is focused on the utility of performance audit for the public or private organization. Included is an examination of the changing input/output relationships necessary for using performance auditing, as well as some actual cases which have resulted in measurable savings from implementing the recommendations of the performance audit. These cases are found in both the private and the public sector, although the public sector has implemented performance audit more pervasively. The cases detail the ways in which performance audits have been used to foster economy, efficiency, and effectiveness in operations. Also in this section, the oversight role of management is considered for both public funds and private firms. Agency theory, which provides a conceptual framework for the managerial stewardship function, provides an explanatory background for the oversight capacity of management, and the auditors' role in assisting management.

The second section takes a look at opportunities to apply accountability reporting. Accountability is relevant in both a macroeconomic sense, and a microeconomic sense. In the macro application, bringing problems of an industry, a nation, or the global village perspective to achieve solutions by a strategic plan are possible, and in fact, achievable. The discussion examines allocation of resources, including the problematic reallocation of technology in a world where redistribution is the rule between nations and states. In the micro environment, a case study is detailed where controversy over two conflicting groups of stakeholders in a private firm is used as an example. The changing needs of input data as well as reported information are explored. Different types of audits which engender different types of control and management reporting are considered.

The third section develops the definitional aspects of the comprehensive performance audit. A distinction is drawn between the traditional audit, and the more pervasive performance audit. The role of the financial, compliance, and operational audits as components of the performance audit is modeled, and the objectives of the performance audit are detailed. Audit evidence, audit report contents, and accountability relationships are demonstrated. The technical aspects of the performance audit are presented. For the manager, an overview of the practice of performance audit is presented. The attestation function of providing audit assurance and an audit opinion is practiced in some nations. In this section, the contextual basis, the investigative basis, and the reporting standards for performance audit are examined. A flowchart analysis of performance audit methodology is displayed for ease in implementing performance audit.

The following section distinguishes between and compares performance audit to the current buzzword techniques of the nineties: reengineering, total quality management, strategic planning, and bottom-up budgeting. Performance auditing is distinct from these techniques, but can be used to enhance the effectiveness of them. In the misguided minds of many, there is sufficient overlap between these management strategies; in organizations where this belief system takes hold, only one technique is used and the results are superficial and temporary. In other organizations, aggressive managements grasp onto so many accountability strategies that operations become confused and unstable. Thus, an exploration of how these strategies can complement each other without overwhelming the need to "do business" will be useful to today's managers.

Because of the significant international differences in the utilization of and methodology for performance audit, a multinational comparison is presented. In addition, needs of multinational firms are reviewed. This discussion constitutes section five. The implementation in different nations has been varied. Some nations have explicit standards for the procedure, scope, and reporting of performance audits; others approach performance auditing on a case by case basis. Still others perform performance audits at the request of external capital providers, such as the United Nations or the International Monetary Fund, in the case of major capital infrastructure projects.

International accounting standards for performance audits do not yet exist. Experiences in nations such as Canada, Australia, New Zealand, Great Britain, the United States, Sweden, Japan, St. Lucia, the Philippines, Thailand and other Asian Organization of Supreme Audit Institution countries, Cyprus, Mexico, and Pakistan are explored. In each set of circumstances, and in each nation, tangible results have been obtained through the practice of performance auditing. This discussion is followed by an analysis of the use of performance auditing by the private firm in a multinational world. The important concepts of risk, accountability relationships, responsiveness, and management oversight are examined in the context of firms with global operations. The unique challenges and opportunities for performance audit in this international setting are investigated.

The final section proceeds with an analysis of conclusions and a summary of the future of value-for-money reporting. The conclusions include demonstration of a pervasive need for the benefits of performance auditing in public, private, and third sector entities. Cost/benefit analysis for applications of performance audit indicate significant success and demonstrable savings. Standardization of procedures, scope, opinions, and reporting in the multinational environment is desirable. Expanding opportunities for the implementation of performance auditing exist, particularly for the use of private external auditors, and particularly in the private sector. The contemporary issues of using performance audit to achieve social responsibility reporting and public interest are considered. Environmental concerns are used as a case example with explicit discussion of practice problems. Also, the future trends of performance audit are explored as standards evolve and standardization of reports enhances comparability of reports for both business and government.

WHAT IS DISTINCTIVE ABOUT A PERFORMANCE AUDIT?

Value-for-money or performance auditing investigates and reports on the economy, efficiency, and effectiveness of operations. It also explores the dimensions of relevance and stability. The technique has been used extensively in the public sector and is becoming an integral part of the audit function in many private sector applications. In a public sector environment where waste and fraud may occur in the presence of dwindling resources and eroding tax bases, the performance audit performs a significant role in identifying the existence of waste and making recommendations for improving the control systems which allowed the waste to occur. It also suggests alternative ways to achieve policy objectives which entail better use of scarce resources. In the private sector, one of the scarce resources is capital, and performance auditing supplements the traditional use of capital budgeting techniques in the capital allocation decisions of management. Demonstrable savings have occurred as a result of performance audit, and managers and auditors alike have become loyal to the technique.

Some have suggested a fourth "e" in addition to economy, efficiency, and effectiveness. This "e" is equity.[10] This dimension causes us to consider the policy itself. Is it appropriate for the State government to concern itself with the municipal commuting habits of the Bay area citizens? Should the State direct the city of San Francisco to revise its car arteries for the purpose of improving air quality, when the city of Los Angeles has a greater proportion of its labor force commuting by car, and its pollution inversions are already legendary? Are the public servants going to be the first to volunteer to get out of their cars and into the mass transit system? While the current status of performance audit takes as its scope the three "e" concepts of economy, efficiency, and effectiveness, the future direction of the technique may include the consideration of equity, i.e., the distribution of goods and services among citizens, states, and nations in the global village. Already, in some nations, program review includes not only the effectiveness dimension, evaluating the success with which the policy objectives are fulfilled, but also includes evaluation of policy itself.

HOW IS PUBLIC POLICY MADE ACCOUNTABLE
BY PERFORMANCE AUDIT?

Performance audit offers the public sector assurance that goods and services are being obtained at the least cost (*economy*), using the most appropriate mix of scarce resources (*efficiency*), which best fulfills the objectives set by elected officials (*effectiveness*). There are many appropriate applications of performance audit in the public sector. Among the most common are audits for the acquisition, utilization, and assignment of assets. Systems which focus on asset safeguards are certainly the most widely used internal control audit objectives in existence.

However, in the traditional audit, asset safeguards and internal control systems fall short of ensuring that assets are bought, used, and allocated in an optimal way. For example, asset acquisition systems may not take into account foreign currency fluctuation, which may affect cost delineation significantly. Asset use may be based on traditional capital budgeting techniques, such as return on investment, but in public arenas, returns may be not be articulated in hard numbers or bottom lines. Other typical capital budgeting techniques, such as accounting rate of return, also have little relevance in the public sector, because, again, desired returns are often outflows rather than inflows. A performance system which tells an organizational unit, "Last year you spent $100 to produce 100 units; this year spend $98," may merely allow the unit to be *less inefficient.*

Performance audit is compatible with the philosophy of the zero-base budgeting system; performance audit is, however, far more comprehensive and workable in its approach. Furthermore, asset allocation optimization requires careful monitoring of capacity, current use, alternative uses, prioritization of objectives, etc. Few internal control or management decision systems have sufficient data, or even sufficiently outlined objectives to assist in the resource allocation problem. Ad hoc decisions, political ramifications, and expediency may drive asset assignment without a proper accounting for the possible effects of misassignment. Performance audit can be used very effectively in these applications.

In addition to asset considerations, the employee work environment is rarely optimized. After all, human resources are not even assets in our current accounting systems. Few public systems have the ability to track the breadth or depth of public servant expertise, and transfers in the system usually come at the initiation of the employee, not the system. A tracking system for managerial personnel is rarely found at all. Systems for accountability of individuals is usually by annual review, which provides too little information, too late, and for too small a proportion of the work force. There are many systems in place for productivity to evaluate labor costs in aggregate for inputs and corresponding outputs; however, service sector productivity for individuals is nearly impossible without detailed specification of qualification inputs, cost inputs, and experience inputs, as related to detailed specification of scheduled outputs. The performance audit process helps to produce the detailed schedules of inputs and outputs that make these productivity systems work, and then further helps to analyze the efficiency of the inputs and the effectiveness of the outputs. Cost reduction goals alone will not work; performance audit evaluates *value* for cost, rather than minimizing cost.

Consider also the difficulty in assessing managerial strategic planning. After the strategic plan is produced, how flexible is it to changes in the external environment? How quickly can the budgets be realigned? Are objectives and outputs easily transformed when the strategic plan is changed? Does the measurement system of inputs and outputs still provide relevant data for performance evaluation? Performance auditing assesses and reports on such information.

Finally, are flexibility and responsiveness maintained within the system? If input costs change unexpectedly, does the organization have the ability to both diagnose the change and respond to it appropriately? If factors external to the firm change the demand for services, does the organization ascertain this information quickly, have a mechanism to provide solutions, and then respond in an appropriate and timely manner? Performance auditing can be of assistance in evaluating the flexibility of the organization, in reviewing the appropriateness of the response to change, and in providing alternatives to suggest to management in various segments of operations. As such, it goes far beyond the requirements of a traditional financial or compliance audit and provides the key assessment of outputs based on given inputs. Furthermore, in most managerial cost systems inputs are accepted as "given" or assumed. Performance audit does not consider inputs as "given," but rather evaluates the inputs directly.

In summary, performance auditing provides relevant feedback to managers, legislators, and private citizens. The utility of the audit is in its reporting on economy, efficiency, and effectiveness. In the case of a public health system, for example, the performance audit will enable the three groups (managers, legislators, citizens) to evaluate whether the medical care which was provided could have been provided at lesser cost, whether there were better systems available or alternative resources available which would have provided the care without sacrificing service, and, finally, whether the public was better off (i.e., healthier) for having had the expenditures made. In a myriad of situations the public sector has successfully used performance auditing and has experienced cost savings far in excess of the cost of the audit itself.

Relevance and Sustainability

Two additional dimensions along which the discussion should continue are relevance and sustainability.[11] The first, relevance, draws direct comparisons between the achievements of a public program and the goals of that program. For example, a goal of reducing the incidence of tuberculosis in homeless shelters may be articulated. In putting in place a medically-supervised program of treatment for TB, medical staff may administer daily doses of a medication which has physical side effects. The homeless, not equipped to deal with the unpleasantness of the treatment, may simply stop using the shelter. Under a traditional goals/achievement measurement, the program goals may appear to be achieved; the incidence of untreated TB among shelter occupants has decreased. The decrease may be dramatic, since only those with symptoms of TB have left the shelter. But the result is not relevant to the goal, and this is the dimension that therefore needs explicit consideration. The infected population is, in effect, worse off rather than improved. The population is largely still untreated.

The last dimension, sustainability, evaluates the stability of program achievements into the future. In the example above, the administration of medication by trained personnel and supervision of the infected population is mandated. But the population is difficult to access; in the long run, some form of outreach programs will be necessary to monitor and evaluate those who are unable to self-administer medication, and to locate and treat newly homeless people.

How successful are current operations in achieving long-term improvements in the incidence of TB in the homeless population? One might be forced to conclude that treatment of today's homeless shelter population has little influence on next year's problems. If this is the case, is the program really efficient, effective, and economical, or is it merely a band-aid for a critical public health problem? Explicit consideration of the sustainability dimension is useful in defining and evaluating assumptions, goals, and achievements over a longer time horizon.

PERFORMANCE AUDIT PRESENTS SOLUTIONS
TO PRIVATE ENTERPRISE

The private sector parallels the needs of the public sector in utility of performance audit with two exceptions: the profit motive may lead to different measurement criteria, and the uncertainty of market realities forces more complexity into the performance audit considerations and reporting elements. However, with relatively minor modification, the performance audit process which has been used so successfully in the public sector, can bring new accountability into the private enterprise. Some areas in which there are particularly rewarding applications include:

- better and more relevant information

- risk analysis

- contingency planning for strategy and also short-run planning

- more effective reporting for better shareholder or regulator visibility of managerial competence

- amplification of reporting of management's productivity which may lead to more efficient capital market allocations

- enhanced independence in the reporting of managerial effectiveness

- an opportunity for firm management to consult freely with outside experts.

Better and More Relevant Information

At a fundamental level, private managers depend upon the reliability, accuracy, and relevancy of the information that is provided to them by staff people. Managers, traditionally involved in planning, directing, and controlling, may not have the time or the expertise to verify the actual data upon which they depend. The control of data accuracy is typically relegated to the internal auditor, who absorbs the key role of implementing, maintaining, and reporting on the viability of the systems of internal control.[12] However, at present, most internal control work hinges on the historical reporting of revenue and cost, and changes in assets, liabilities, and cash flows. In this application, while the integrity of the financial reporting system is crucial to the manager, the nonfinancial data, and in particular, the "soft" data needs of managers, may not be adequately addressed. This area, the examination of "soft" data needs for managers, from prospective reports of firm performance to macroeconomic forecasting, is a key area for effective managerial decision making. The improvement of "soft" data requirements for management will clearly enhance the economy, efficiency, and effectiveness of the strategic planners in both the short run and the long run. Internal auditors exert a strong marginal contribution by initiating systems of internal control for nonfinancial nonhistorical data systems.

Analysis of Risk

The analysis of risk is a critical component of performance and accountability assessment. Explicit evaluation of potential risk and past risks provides management with the tools for cost/benefit analysis, as well as the keystones for strategic planning of accountability reporting. By defining risk, management can plan for contingencies. They are able to react faster and more effectively to changes in both external and internal events. Another benefit of risk assessment is that the firm is led to measure the sensitivity of financial, growth, and other goals to external events such as regulatory intervention, tax policy changes, health care plan overhaul, raw material supply disruptions, and others. For example, public firms now report expanded discussions of managerial goals in annual reports. The enhancement of the "management, discussion, and analysis" section of the annual report has come after extensive Securities and Exchange Commission rulings and hearings. Essentially, existing and potential shareholders were felt to be disadvantaged in capital market decisions by the focus in annual reports on financial data. The public, it was felt, would be better served by some forward-looking, narrative, "soft" data with which to assess the future performance of the firm.

However, corporate directors and managers have met this challenge with severe trepidation. They have wondered how many lawsuits would arise from unmet expectations. They are worried about how many unions would take advantage in wage negotiations when the firm profitability was reported to be rosy in the future. They have experienced anxiety that if a very positive outlook on growth in market share were reported, it would be taken as a signal by competitors to enter their market. The risk for the firm is for reporting positive information. It is rare for a lawsuit to be brought against a firm which provided unexpectedly high returns for an investor, or returns which were in excess of projections. Rather, troubles stem from failure to meet reported expectations. Shareholders go after firms who fail to deliver on reported expectations. This situation produces a reporting situation where there is a bias toward underreporting expectation, where conservatism reigns. In turn, these lowered or modest corporate reports of future performance are often taken in the international capital market as weakness or vulnerability of American business growth. In turn, then, international capital may turn away from American business.

Performance auditing techniques allow firms to assess those risks which are most likely to influence growth, profitability, market share, and other performance indicators in the future. In reporting these risk factors corporations are better able to inform the public why goals may not be achieved. The investment community is then better able to make realistic decisions and understand the inherent risk of projections.

There are certainly many areas in which risk analysis is significant for firms. Liability for products must be built into the pricing system for drugs by the pharmaceutical industry. The increasing instability in tax policy leaves firms unable to plan effectively for long-run capital projects and leaves many firms vulnerable to takeovers. Furthermore, the more information which is disclosed to the public on positive performance of business segments, the more competitors seize opportunities to enter newly profitable markets. The use of comprehensive and broad risk analysis fosters good reporting, good planning, and better flexibility in adjusting strategic plans to current conditions.

Contingency Planning

Contingency planning is an augmentation of the risk analysis process. Contingency plans are characterized by the evaluation of internal structure, rather than the external structure which is the focus of the risk analysis. Contingency plans are one facet of the evaluation of management's success in meeting stated objectives. Contingency planning is useful in place of the technique of management by objectives, which is more directed toward steering management toward goal attainment, and which tends to operate in a flat dimension (asking were objectives attained)? Contingency planning involves a deeper analysis by asking, "Could the objectives have been attained better by following an alternative management strategy?" That is, the effectiveness and efficiency dimensions are added to management by objectives in the implementation of contingency planning. Instead of asking whether objectives were met at least cost, the questions are directed toward whether the objectives could have been met better. And further, it asks whether the stated objectives were appropriate given the resources employed.

The management axiom of the 1980s was, "Success is being able to implement Plan B." In the 1990s, success is being measured by both flexibility and fast reactions to changing conditions. In the twenty-first century, producing quality Plan B alternatives quickly will be critical to respond to global challenges. These conditions may relate to suppliers, consumers, regulation, taxation, mergers, or reduced profitability. The management who meets success head on will be that team who has a balanced portfolio of alternatives ready when circumstances dictate change. Perhaps most significantly, performance audit fosters explicit delineation of alternatives, sensitivity analysis, and planning.

Enhanced Reporting for Visibility of Management

Certainly, professionals have been active in improving the quality and diversity of reporting in the public and private sectors. The accountancy professional has been particularly concerned with enhanced disclosure. The American Institute of Certified Public Accountants' Public Oversight Board of the SEC Practice Section issued a report in 1993 significantly titled, *In the Public Interest: Issues Confronting the Accounting Profession.*[13] The report demonstrates the profession's commitment to continued improvement in financial and management reporting. While a considerable portion of the report addresses recommendations for litigation reform which would limit auditor liability, it also confronts the system of financial reporting.

The AICPA took a leadership role in oversight of financial reporting in 1977 by the initiation of a peer review program for audit firms practicing with SEC clients. Even so, an "expectations gap" exists in the role of auditors and financial reports. The gap refers to the difference between what auditors are doing to insure the reporting of integrity, accuracy, and completeness of financial reports, and what the public perceives is the auditor's job.

This gap became wider in the 1980s as the burgeoning economy dealt with an unprecedented number of innovative business dealings, creative reporting, new financial instruments, and new ways of structuring and restructuring asset acquisitions. In fact, the existing financial reporting rules simply were not applicable in many cases to the innovative budgeting, business management, and reporting situations created by the new economic surge. The confidence of the public in reading reports of business and government eroded as business failures and city budget crises escalated.

The 1993 report provides concrete expectations for the profession. These include mandated disclosures of risk and uncertainty, increased discussion of the nature of "estimates" in reported financial figures, and enhanced responsibility for the detection and disclosure reporting errors or misstatements. In addition, the report addresses the nature of the relationship between the auditor and his client. Along this dimension, direction is provided to the auditor to avoid the appearance of impaired objectivity, and to avoid a consulting relationship with a client which may appear to the public to impair an auditor's objectivity.

Of particular concern in achieving accountability is the improvement of corporate governance. For publicly held companies, audit committees are playing a more significant role in cultivating financial statements which elucidate the economy, efficiency, and effectiveness dimensions. Internal control within organizations continues to be the primary mechanism for achieving sustainable management effectiveness, and reporting on the adequacy of management's concern with economy and efficiency. The performance audit integrates constructively with these enhanced reporting trends.

Finally, the addition of an audit opinion on the performance audit, would further augment the integrity of the reporting process and foster better capital markets. In order for the practice of rendering an opinion on performance audit reports to progress further developments will have to take place in the setting of standards for the performance, scope, and reporting of performance audits. However, as the claims for scarce resources continue to escalate, public demands for better accountability in both the public and the private sector will drive the evolution of the practice of performance audit. Furthermore, the trend in reporting away from traditional financial reporting to increased focus on qualitative and forward-looking information will most surely affect the demand for performance audit, which is able to handle the nonquantitative aspects of reporting from management.

Better Shareholder/Citizen Awareness of Management Performance for Improved Public Policy and Capital Market Efficiency

In the public sector, ineffective management leads to dysfunctional spending and inappropriate distribution of wealth among citizens. This, in turn, leads citizens to become disenchanted with public leadership; they then vote out the ineffective leaders and replace them with effective ones. So goes the theory of regulation. But does the system work?

Disenchantment of the "the system" in municipal, local, state, and federal bureaucracy is at a high mark. A different sort of "expectations gap" may be the culprit here, and what is the solution? Enhanced reporting to the public. The gap corresponds to the public's desire to spend less and get more. This rational behavior is endemic to us all, regardless of income level. The rationality of the behavior, however, is dependent upon a somewhat detailed and explicit understanding of the sources and uses of public funds, and a personal conviction about public priorities. Take as an example, the public school administration in your area. For you to be a rational decision maker, you must have access to a comprehensible but concise set of data which includes who is providing funding, and who is receiving it. Then you will want to see expenditures and have an understanding of how these relate to your personal convictions about public priorities. Finally, you want some assurance that resources were obtained at least cost, and that they were not squandered, so that you can assess your desire to retain or dispose of the existing public officials. What we have, of course, is your need to know the effectiveness, efficiency, and economy of management, as well as its sustainability. But you are challenged to obtain this information from existing disclosures! The complexity, aggregation, and fund accounting systems are working against you. Thus, in order to coax the "system" to work in the public sector, improved management accountability information is critical.

In the private sector a different but equally compelling argument may be made. The role of financial and management reporting is to assist capital providers in making decisions about where capital should be placed. The success and sustainability of the free market system is dependent on capital flowing to effective organizations. If capital flows to effective organizations, they will grow and succeed; if capital flows to ineffective organizations, waste and ineffective production and services are tolerated. If capital flows to the ineffective organizations the market is "inefficient." The critical factor, once again, is relevant, timely, and comprehensive information regarding the operations of management and financial reports. Continued reporting of decision-relevant information permits capital providers to withhold, commit, or move their capital from firm to firm based on performance reports. Thus, the capital market maintains its effectiveness.

In recent years public reporting of corporate operations has encountered a prolific expansion. In addition to audited financial information, increased "soft" (i.e., projected or nonfinancial) data and unaudited data is mandated. The Management Discussion and Analysis section of the annual report made to stockholders has been significantly expanded by Securities and Exchange Commission requirements, including improved comparability, forward-looking assessments, and greater depth in management reporting.

Overall, capital markets are well-served by better information which enables investors to make reliable capital market decisions. The purpose of the expanded disclosures is not to diminish the inherent riskiness of the capital market, but rather to better enable investors to assess risk and invest along their personal risk preferences. In a similar vein, the performance audit reports further clarify, diversify, and add depth to existing disclosures about the management's oversight of a firm. This further augments the efficiency of capital markets.

Independence in Reporting on Management Operations

Performance audit techniques and performance audit reporting add standardization to the format of corporate and public sector disclosures. As the public sector continues to proliferate the type and number of performance audits, readers of disclosures have come to expect augmented management reports. The performance audit intensifies this effort, as external parties are called upon to evaluate and report on the oversight of management. This elevated disclosure, when combined with the added independence from management in using external auditors, provides assurance to capital providers, be they taxpayers or investors, that the reports are free from material misstatement. Enhanced reliance on the reporting system, in turn, justifies its increased costs by providing increased benefits.

An Opportunity to Consult with Outsiders

In several applications, particularly in Canada, utilities have set up teams to be exchanged between firms for the purpose of assessing managerial effectiveness. This sort of peer review acts to supplement audit information with industry expectations. Furthermore, audit committees which act to engage and define the role of auditors within firms, provide a helpful distancing between consultants retained by management and outsiders called in as auditors to scrutinize performance measures. This distancing benefits the independence desired between managers and investors and adds to the integrity of information.

RETHINKING INFORMATION INPUTS AND OUTPUTS
FOR EFFECTIVE PERFORMANCE AUDIT

Some of the facets of performance we would like to be able to scrutinize will require revisions of information inputs and outputs. The traditional complaints about accounting information inadequacies when compared to true "economic" costs and benefits are particularly relevant here. Cost of capital is rarely used in reporting, with the exception of capital budgeting for capital expenditures. But many other nonfixed asset uses of capital fail to consider and account for opportunity costs, for example. Furthermore, costs external to the reporting entity may be overlooked. Consider an example.

A low-cost, highly productive and available work force Puerto Rico paired with extensive tax advantages has led to rapid economic development. In particular, many pharmaceutical firms have found conditions so favorable there that they have become a significant economic presence. As they have absorbed the work force, provided previously unavailable fringe benefits, and steadily increased base wages, social problems have escalated. Increasing affluence of some has caused massive discontent of others. Crime, drug problems, industrial pollution, demands for increasing taxes to improve social safety nets have accelerated. This, in turn, causes costs of business operations to rise, forcing pharmaceutical plants to consider relocating elsewhere, sometimes in Caribbean nations which still offer the advantages Puerto Rico once did. What has gone sour here?

This is simply an example of strategic reporting gone soft. The costs reported are the traditional accounting costs which are firm-specific. The "costs" underreported are those which are macro rather than micro in focus. Even while complying with existing pollution laws, effluent warmer than the surrounding ocean from the plants is killing local reefs south of the island. Tourism and the tropical fish export industry suffer, as does commercial fishing. The costs reported by the firm are firm-specific. They do not include the longer-term, environmental and social impacts. This situation persists even in view of *compliance audits* which report on the firm's adherence to relevant laws, regulations, and procedures. True performance reporting enables firms to cast a wide net in their assessment of operations, and enhances long-term strategic planning.

Another example of a traditionally unreported cost pertains to timeliness. In the private sector, failure to initiate a new product line may be costly. In the public sector delay in beginning a social program may represent an unreported but significant cost. A public sector example will be relevant here.

A vaccine (MMR) to prevent the occurrence of measles has been inexpensively and readily available for decades. As vaccination became routine, the incidence of the disease became insignificant. However, vaccinations are preventive, as opposed to being related to a diagnosis of illness; a diagnosis is required in most insurance and public assistance programs. Perceiving minimal risk, those who suffered from either poverty or tight-fistedness did not pursue vaccination. The result was an enormous increase of measles outbreaks in all levels of schools, even requiring some university closings. Public policy now generally requires evidence of inoculation for school attendance. In this example, reporting was the solution. However, the performance issues remain buried in the data: what were the costs of not reporting earlier? How much is spent on compliance assurance? How much is saved by eradicating measles outbreaks? By framing the financial questions by performance objectives, new cost/benefit relationships emerge. Both input and output data needs to be specified carefully if performance audits are to be truly relevant.

HOW PERFORMANCE AUDIT IS BEING USED
FOR TANGIBLE RESULTS

Financial controls are accepted without question in both the public and the private sector. In most situations, control is accomplished by a system of internal control which exposes unauthorized or inefficient use of funds or other assets. The value of performance auditing is clear in circumstances where the outputs cannot be related to the inputs on a dollar for dollar basis. The dollar to dollar comparison is not always valid, even in the private sector, where a profit motive is assumed. Productivity is often measured in dollars and hours spent working (input measures) to goods or services provided (output measures). Take, for example, a recently reported case wherein an inspector general in the third sector (quasi-public) found a dangerous form of inefficiency in a large metropolitan area. His staff found a troubling increased response time among the emergency medical service (ambulance) tracking system. The system distributes patients and ambulances within the geographic area and among the participating medical care providers, such as emergency clinics or hospital emergency rooms. Subsequent to a comprehensive audit, the problem was found. It did not relate to unauthorized expenditures. Costs were in control, as were the number of outputs, with the exception of response time. Nor was there productivity decline due to personnel absence or turnover, or lengthy breaks away from the computer terminal. Rather, operators were spending *too much* time at the terminal. On the computer system was an unauthorized sex software game called Foreplay; it not only was taking the operators away from their assigned duties, but also exposed the computer system to the introduction of viruses (we are assuming computer viruses, not physically-transmitted kinds of viruses).

In observing the uses of performance audit, it must be noted that the scope and reporting process for the performance audit varies widely across applications. Nevertheless, the results have been useful to the auditee, and accountability has been enhanced. While more prevalent in the public sector at present, performance auditing is spreading into the private sector as well.

PERFORMANCE AUDITING ENHANCES OVERSIGHT

Capital Market Efficiency

The theory of efficient capital markets instructs us that management will be reasonably objective in assessing performance of their organizations. For example, if management is too optimistically biased in their reports, recipients of this overly favorable information will intuitively deflate management's reports in following periods. Similarly, if management is overly pessimistic, financial report readers will inflate this conservative assessment in future periods.[14] Thus, there is little or no incentive except in the very short run for management to bias financial reports or other public information to citizens or shareholders. Another facet of efficient markets on publicly disclosed information concerns the nature of data reported. The theory predicts that if corporations and governments would be rewarded in the marketplace for disclosing information, they would do so, even in the absence of regulations, since they would benefit from such disclosures. In addition, if the marketplace desired information which was not readily available, the theory would predict that citizens or investors would undertake the discovery costs to obtain the information, either in a public or private way. Unfortunately, here, the theory does not hold up so well. We know, for example, that investors value disclosures on performance of segments within large diversified companies. However, corporations, fearing entry of competitors into markets where profitability is above average, consider this information proprietary. This is a situation where corporations will resist and lobby against increased disclosures.

The system of efficiency of information in capital markets works well where there are benefits to both disclosing parties and information seekers. The system works less well where information seekers may benefit at the expense of discloser. So, the failure of accountability is not really in the oft cited lack of integrity of the information reported; integrity of information is very high, and the incidence of audit failure is extremely small. Rather, the failure of accountability is more in the realm of what is reported, how it is presented, and with what frequency it is disseminated. Most would agree that the quality and quantity of financial reporting is very high in the United States. But many will also complain that the costs of presenting data and interpreting it are exorbitant to preparers and users alike. Furthermore, accountability dimensions are either particularly absent from public information or particularly challenging to obtain. Performance auditing reports fill this gap.

The Stewardship Function and Capital Markets

Another factor in the economics of information and its effect upon accountability relates to "agency costs." Agency costs arise due to the fact that citizens, in the case of governments, and shareholders, in the case of firms, delegate by necessity decisions about running organizations to managers. Citizens and capital providers are not able, or not willing, or not competent, to run governments and businesses themselves. Managers are thus the "agents" for citizens and shareholders. However, because there is distance between the citizens/shareholders and managers, costs such as those pertaining to financial reporting and other disclosures are incurred. In recent cases, unfortunately, there are instances of managers acting in self-interest rather than in the interest of those they represent. This increases "agency costs," particularly if the behavior persists over time. Moreover, since many compensation arrangements for corporate officers are dependent upon short-range criteria, such as the current year's earnings-per-share growth, managers may have systemic incentives to sacrifice long-term growth for short-run increases in earnings. In the public sector, one does not have to strain to recall some well-publicized instances in which government officials acted unchecked in self-interest. Consider, for example, the House banking scandal in which representatives routinely overdrafted personal accounts which were then covered by public funds; or consider less obvious malintentioned examples, such as the existence of a private and subsidized barber shop for Congress, when Washington exhibits no shortage of convenient and low-cost barber shops. Or consider, also, that Congress routinely exempts itself from the complex and costly labor regulations which they impose on the rest of us; the recently enacted Americans with Disabilities Act, for example, will not apply to Congress. The value of any kind of audit, whether it is a financial audit, operational audit, compliance audit, or performance audit is in the audit's value in communicating to the citizens/shareholders that managers are operating effectively in their interests. Performance audits, in particular, reduce agency costs by providing assurance in a clear and relevant manner that managers are making decisions in which economy, efficiency, and effectiveness are sustained. The signals that the performance audit provides to consumers of information then provide a mechanism for citizens or shareholders to increase or withhold funds, or to push for a change in management. The level of independence of the performance audit further assures the public that management is not biasing information.

Performance audits decrease agency costs by exposing management decisions to independent and external evaluations of concern for economy, efficiency, and effectiveness of programs. The audit provides independent evidence that the reports are reliable and relevant, and provide a convenient mechanism for principals to evaluate their agents in a direct, as opposed to an inferential manner. In this way, accountability and improved control are achieved as managers openly report on the impact of their decisions. The mere existence of a performance audit policy causes managers to reflect on their compliance with programmatic objectives, knowing that public reports will bring management actions into the sunshine. Performance reporting acts as an incentive for managers to better serve those for whom they act as agents.

NOTES

1. U.S. House of Representatives. Committee on Government Operations. *Managing the Federal Government: A Decade of Decline.* 1993.

2. "23 Years into EPA's Mandate, Public Protection Seen Lacking." *The Washington Post,* May 24, 1993, A:17.

3. *House Report on Government Operations.* 1993.

4. Brian Kelly. *Adventures in Porkland: How Washington Wastes Your Money and Why They Won't Stop.* New York: Villard Books. 1993; also, Martin L. Gross. *The Government Racket: Washington Waste From A to Z.* New York: Bantam Books. 1993.

5. The Association of Certified Fraud Examiners. *The White Paper*, 7: 2 (April–May 1993): 25.

6. Thomas P. Kelley. "The COSO Report: Challenge and Counterchallenge." *Journal of Accountancy* (February 1993): 10–18.

7. *The White Paper*, 24.

8. *The White Paper*, 24.

9. *The White Paper*, 25.

10. D. R. Sheldon and E. F. McNamara. *Value-for-Money Auditing in the Public Sector*. Altamonte Springs, FL: Institute of Internal Auditors Research Foundation. 1991.

11. See, for example, the model presented by Dennis Duquette and Alexis M. Stowe, "A Performance Measurement Model for the Office of the Inspector General." *Government Accountants Journal* (Summer 1993): 27–49.

12. See, for example, *Standards for the Professional Practice of Internal Auditing*, The Institute of Internal Auditors.

13. AICPA, SEC Practice Section, Public Oversight Board. *In the Public Interest: Issues Confronting the Accounting Profession*. New York: AICPA. New York. 1993.

14. There is extensive research on whether markets are efficient for financial information. Most research indicates that markets are, in fact, relatively efficient, but find asymmetry in market reaction to overly positive and overly negative reports of management.

Chapter 2

Opportunities to Apply Accountability

INTRODUCTION

Accountability involves at least three critical dimensions. First, the organization must know their client base. Second, they must be able to measure client satisfaction with the organization's goods or services. Third, they must have a set of ready, responsive, measurable reactions when client satisfaction declines. "Performance" is the net which captures all three elements. Organizations can only perform well if they understand to whom they respond and serve. Then, they need to know the extent to which their performance is successful. When they fall short on performance, the implementation of contingency plans to improve performance should be swift and monitored diligently. If, then, these three elements come together coherently, performance is achieved, and the organization is accountable to its customers, clients, or stakeholders.

Accountability reporting is achieved when the three elements of performance are combined with the three major elements of comprehensive audit: economy (least cost), efficiency (best combination of scarce resource use), and effectiveness (fulfilling organizational goals). That is, the performance elements are disclosed on the basis of the audit dimensions to afford public use of the information. Clearly, the more standardized the presentation, the more easily comparability between organizations is assessed. Unfortunately, standardization of reporting dimensions is difficult, particularly between different industries in the private sector and different sizes of government units in the public sector. This is both because of organizational complexity as well as diverse organizational goals among units.

Accountability is more difficult to achieve in the public sector than in the private sector, but is complex in both contexts. In this chapter, the opportunity to apply accountability through performance auditing in the public sector is explored first; then, the discussion is expanded to the private sector. Next, the relationships between the performance audit and other audits are delineated. Finally, performance audit scope is considered, as well as globally useful analytical constructs. "Global" here applies to both the ability to apply performance audit across industries and governments, as well as its applicability in the international arena. In the next chapter, implementation mechanisms are surveyed.

USING PERFORMANCE AUDIT IN MANAGING SOCIAL CONFLICT: A MACRO CASE

There have been many attempts to measure performance in the public sector, and yet still citizens decry the lack of accountability, the waste, the fraud, and the self-serving actions of public officials and their staffs. Focus has been on two facets of the problem: first, defining outputs of local, state and federal governments and agencies is problematic. Second, satisfying constituencies or stakeholders who have competing interests requires intense lobbying by the stakeholders, compromise, and good public relations and information dissemination by the public officials. In other words, golden benefits to one constituent group are considered wasted by an unaffected or disinterested group. We can look at this in "macro" terms by focusing on world problems, or in relatively "micro" terms by decisions made in a more limited arena. Let's look at the macro environment first.

A significant potential use of performance auditing is present in the management of international social conflict. In this evolving context a technique which assesses economy, efficiency, and effectiveness of activities offers material and measurable benefits. The result of issuing a performance audit report serves to signal interested parties and constituent groups of the extent to which the activity was performed for the least cost (economy), used the most efficient combination of scarce resources (efficiency), and achieved stated objectives (effectiveness).[1] Performance auditing has, in fact, been implemented in some government operations, some private corporations, internationally in selected World Bank and United Nations projects, as well as several other national government operations.

Consider, for example, the objective of achieving world peace. Increasingly, peace involves not just avoiding or ending armed confrontation, but rather calls to redistribute wealth between and within nations. This wealth transfer encompasses direct cash aid and loan guarantees, goods and services, and technology transfer. This redistribution requires political lobbying, citizen support, and extensive monitoring. Support, consent, and monitoring could be significantly enhanced by the use of performance auditing for accountability in the management of this redistribution to avoid social conflict. The enhancement is the result of signaling and monitoring mechanisms between parties in the wealth transfer process. It is not difficult to integrate the knowledge and practice of performance auditing into the arena of international peace activities.

A fundamental change in the sources of conflict will be observed in the next century. Conflicts will increasingly be the result of clashes over goods, services, and technology, and decreasingly the result of fighting over land and boundaries. This is inevitable as technology provides mechanisms to enhance the superproduction of food and consumer goods. It will be less important to hold land, than to hold technology.

Combined with this vision is a critical need for peoples and nations to manage the environment and to coordinate maintenance of the planet's water, air, and natural resources. Those who hold technology to control and combat pollution are targets of those less wealthy who must victimize their own natural resources to provide essential goods and services for their populace. Housing needs will be changed dramatically by the ability to manage energy. Production facilities will be changed by an increasing ability to transfer information and communicate by remote access.

An Innovative Application

The coming century will encounter, then, an increased need to redistribute wealth and to coordinate resource maintenance across national boundaries. Failure to achieve equilibrium in the transfers of wealth and resource maintenance will inevitably lead to international conflict. Allocation procedures, public policy, government oversight, and economic analyses will be played out in this new arena. What techniques are potentially useful in the resolution of these conflicts, and how can they be introduced in a timely manner to deter confrontation?

Different methodologies are responsive to the different types of economics in the transfer of wealth. For example, it is hypothesized above that the "new economics" which will operate in the following century is the "economics of need." There is an awakening in this new field of economics of need, which addresses the taxonomy of needs: normative need (as we now define transfers of aid based on expert opinion), perceived need (as described by those in need), and comparative need (as designated by relationships of wealth between competing sectors).[2] An innovative potential use of the new concept of performance audit may offer significant advantages to the management of international social confrontation. Essentially, we can view the objective of peace maintenance through management of transfers as the operationalization of "value for money." This is the objective of performance auditing. Performance auditing is a process of identifying strategic objectives, acting to meet the objectives, and measuring the objectives. It reports on economy (achieving at least cost), efficiency (achieving by using an optimal allocation of scarce resources), and effectiveness (measuring success in meeting objectives). Social audit may be of benefit in predicting, managing, and reporting on social confrontation.[3] The integration of performance auditing into the management of social confrontation interfaces the literature of accounting and auditing, economics, foreign policy, and regulation.

An Instructive Case

We have a successful classroom exercise we call "The Jelly Bean Wars." Students are divided into groups, and each group represents a continent. Each group is given black jelly beans to represent cash, green jelly beans to represent foodstuffs, white jelly beans to represent consumer goods, and yellow jelly beans to represent new technology. (Now you know why accountants are called "bean counters.") Parallel to reality, some continents are given many jelly beans, some very few, and all are given differing amounts of each color corresponding to continent wealth. The objective is for the groups to negotiate to improve their continent's wealth. The post-negotiating discussion is structured to have the participants recognize (a) that they demanded information and evidence or corroboration of information in order to make a jelly bean grant or exchange, and (b) how they monitored the subsequent exchanges, including forcing groups to disclose "need" and "existing wealth."

Similar to the jelly bean wars, we may use what we know about wealth transfers, information, accountability, and needs assessment, and integrate this knowledge into a new model of accountability. It is known that transfers are more likely to take place if the donor has "insurance" that the recipient will use the transfer economically, efficiently, and effectively. As social conflict is ever more likely to cause intra- and international confrontation in the future, this transfer process has a significant need to be explored.

This process draws upon several multidisciplinary theoretical constructs. Utilization of the economics literature contributes the concept of wealth transfer utility and the decision-making process of reallocation. This literature is extensive, but lacks the perspective of accountability and reporting for wealth transfers. The accounting and auditing literature focuses on the integrity of financial reporting, the maintenance of costs, and the signalling value (i.e., information economics) of audited reports.

The theory of regulation adds the dimension of social utility, and this literature addresses the political process of redistributions. Finally, the foreign policy literature offers the concepts of international equity considerations and protection of national interest in an interdependent world. Integration of these fields holds promise for defining and communicating accountability for aid projects.

Accountability Needs Good Information

Capital flows and transfer of technology are dependent upon a political process which assigns priorities for need, often based on avoidance of social conflict or conflict resolution. These flows, in turn, are the result of information flows. When information is inaccurate, incomplete, or difficult to interpret, flows are hampered. Deserving projects may be unfunded or underfunded. Accountability information needs to be accessible and easily interpreted by all participants in the political process: taxpayers, elected officials, private providers, and governmental professionals. Performance auditing poses a meaningful model for information transfer integrating performance auditing techniques to monitor the appropriation and use of funds.

The Theory in the Macro Model

We are drawing on several theoretical models. Agency theory literature in finance and accounting involves investigation of why the public values audits. The value is due to the "insurance" provided by audit assurance that the nonowner "agents" (managers) are protecting the interests of the owners.[4] Information theory addresses the benefits of better decision making and risk reduction due to the appropriate amount, timeliness, and quality of information.[5] Economics and foreign policy issues are dealt with in Keynesian multiplier theory. As noted in the theoretical literature, two fundamental questions in the implementation of the multiplier are definitional issues and data issues. Underlying all of these is the theoretical literature on stewardship theory, addressing accountability associated with the gap produced by having others spend an individual owner's resources.[6]

Nonprofit Entities

Accountability in nonprofit organizations is often elusive. The measurement and disclosure of results is a diverse as the organizations themselves. Even when economy, efficiency, and effectiveness are achieved, it is difficult for the public to measure.

Many times accountability is an evasive goal. For example, Philadelphia's municipal management estimated that its deficit for the year 1991 would be sixty million; however, Moody's assessed the deficit at $180 million.[7] Similarly, even top-flight universities have allowed accountability problems to persist, failing to address changing demographics, economic conditions, and employment trends; dramatic programmatic shifts were enacted at Columbia University, whose 1993 deficit was around $83 million, and Yale and Stanford faced similar downsizing and cuts to address deficits.[8]

THE PRIVATE SECTOR: A MICRO CASE

Now, let's consider a more micro example, this time in the private sector, again looking at the combination of theoretical constructs which are useful in predicting and explaining the nature of accountability and performance reporting. Recently, the Marriott Corporation, well known for relatively tight management and effective growth, took actions which brought great controversy upon the reputation of the company, as well as accusations of unethical behavior. It may be years before the shareholders and bondholders sort out in court the issues of this management's actions. Here is the history of the management crisis and the ensuing accountability dilemma.

In early 1991, Marriott Corporation found itself in the unenviable position of having to reassure its investors that the $8.3 billion company was not, in fact, going down the tubes. In effect, they supplied the financial press with the information that the weak demand for hotel and related services was responsible for poor performance, not management actions. By late 1991, however, Moody's dropped Marriott's debt ratings, assessing the poor real estate and hotel sale market's effects on the corporation. In October, 1992, Marriott Corporation disclosed that it would split into two companies. William R. Tiefel, the president of the Marriott Lodging Group, explained that the plan to split the company would improve services and ultimately improve profitability.[9]

An Accountability Controversy

However, depending on which stakeholder was talking, some characterized the split as creating two companies: one "good" and one "bad." Marriott investors began to threaten lawsuits to prevent the planned summer 1993 division. The plan initially was to create two new corporations, "Marriott International" and "Host-Marriott." The management purpose was to shore up poor shareholder returns and reduce an unwieldy debt. The hotel management group (Marriott International), generally in the hotel, restaurant, food services industry, would be in strong financial shape, shed of debt, while the flagging real estate and retirement community operations would become Host-Marriott, taking over the debt burdens. The high growth hotel services group would be winners; the risky real estate/property group would be losers. In effect, the ability to pay off the debt, given that the profitable operations had been split off into a separate entity was drawn into question.

Investors did not stand still. Rather, in October 1992 senior debt holders representing over $120 million in bonds filed suit, complaining that Marriott had not adequately warned debtholders of their plan. A committee representing the debt holders was formed, including pension plan managers and other institutional investors, to fight the split. But by November of that year, a federal judge decreed that all bondholder interests should be combined into one suit. Merrill Lynch & Co., who was working with Marriott on the split-up as an advisor, became uncomfortable with the liability and announced its departure from the project. Its departure did not protect it however. IDS Financial Services accused Merrill Lynch of improper behavior for having put the firm's assets heavily into Marriott. At issue, in part, were complaints from debtholders that when $400 million in bonds were issued in the Spring of 1992, Marriott failed to disclose the split-up plans. In fact, by Spring of 1993 a judge had ruled that investors were permitted to bring securities fraud accusations against Marriott.

J. Willard Marriott, Chairman and President, reasoned that segregation of the healthy from the unhealthy in the firm would permit the entire entity to move forward. Many realistically felt, however, that one of the new entities was taking the assets, while the other took the liabilities. The plan to split caused two groups to benefit differentially: stock rose more than ten percent in the first year of the plan, helping equity investors, while the bonds were downgraded, hurting debt investors. As Marriott continued to negotiate with the warring factions, some preferred-equity investors, holding 2.1 million shares, decided to fight the corporation split, as preferred dividends would be curtailed under the new arrangement. In effect, the traditional position of preferred and common stockholders would be reversed; under the Marriott plan, common shareholders would be paid dividends before compensating preferred shareholders.

By June of 1993, the Securities and Exchange Commission had approved the plan to split. At the same time, reported corporate profitability took a plunge from a massive $32 million real estate write-off on unsold hotels. In September 1993, the firm announced that the restructuring would be tax-free for Marriott International. The negotiated settlement provided a one-for-one swap of Marriott International Stock for the old Marriott Corporation stock. Marriott countered preferred shareholder and bondholder arguments with the observation that the stock price in Fall of 1993, of the two new entities combined, had doubled from the 1992 stock price of the single entity.

Effects Seen in the Capital Market

The 1993 revised plan was to retire the outstanding bonds of Marriott corporation in exchange for a new combination of $1.5 billion in cash, stocks, and newly issued bonds. Because the new plan offered some remunerative rewards to the dissidents, an agreement was reached; but the suit on failure to disclose prior to the 1992 bond issue remained.

Again, Marriott's stock rose. Standard & Poors announced that a strong rating would be applied to Marriott International's bonds. In all, almost 90 percent of the debt of Marriott was to be exchanged in the deal. To allay fears, the Marriott family agreed to maintain a 25 percent interest in each of the spun-off companies.

The Marriott restructuring affected the multinational investment climate, with some bondholders calling for new restrictive covenants to prevent stripping debt from operations. There are those who feel cheated, and those who would accuse management of sacrificing bondholder interests in favor of equity holders. As many management incentive plans are stock-based, these accusations extend to claims that management is self-serving in a company split which benefits stockholders. On the other hand, the financial health of the "healthy unit" improved dramatically, and forecasts predict that even Host Marriott will turn a profit by the end of 1994.[10]

In evaluating the Marriott Corporation example, it is apparent that many stakeholders were affected, as well as the general public. Some of these stakeholders are firm management (several of whom were summarily replaced during the negotiations), bondholders, stockholders, accountants, attorneys, as well as outsiders: customers, suppliers, creditors, institutional investors including pension fund investors and holders, and brokerage firms.

Traditional financial statements, even with a management discussion and analysis section, would not have adequately portrayed the effects of management decisions on these stakeholders. A traditional financial audit at year end would have provided some insight into the riskiness of the changes, and the question of whether the entity was a "going concern" would be addressed. Proxy statements also serve to notify the public of significant events.

But even with this full array of extensive public disclosures, several parties of stakeholders accused the firm of misleading them, even while the firm was in material compliance with disclosure policy: bondholders, brokers, underwriters, financial institutions, and others found themselves clamoring for more information, and more timely information, from management. And, all too often in recent controversies, the accounting profession has found itself the party of last resort, the deep pockets when aggrieved stakeholders want redress.

Accountants and Risk

As such, the accountants find the liability of "doing business" increasingly high. The frequency and awards in such cases are escalating, including multiple millions in settlements. Like obstetricians whose malpractice premiums squeezed their income causing them to change specialties, at least one large regional public accounting firm has been bankrupted by litigation, and fears of a major firm dissolving persist.[11] In the *Special Report by the Public Oversight Board* of the AICPA, it is noted that the auditor's report carries a major financial benefit to investors in the capital market, and reliance upon it serves to shore up the marketplace.

Unfortunately, these escalating cases of litigation, and the often absurdly high "damages" which accounting firms are ordered to pay to make restitution, have the effect of curbing the amount and type of information that accountants are willing to evaluate. On the other hand, there is the need for management to maintain a highly innovative nature in an increasingly brutal competitive financial marketplace. The spiraling and dynamic nature of inventive financial instruments and transactions makes enhancement of the amount and type of disclosures even more critical for efficient capital markets. The Marriott case illustrates this clash of the pull for increased disclosure on the part of the public, and resistance to it from corporations (especially directors) and auditors who are increasingly the blame of last resort.

In fact, the Public Oversight Board has taken an active role in facing the challenges of this dilemma. More effort is being put forth to help the public understand the intrinsic limits of audit reports, financial statements, and detection of management fraud. In addition, public relations efforts are underway. These emphasize the difference between business failure and audit failure. Business failure may be due to management ineffectiveness, but is also often due to change in macroeconomic conditions over which management may exercise minimal control. Audit failure occurs when the auditors fail to adhere to the codified statements of auditing procedure resulting in a misleading audit report.

Disclosure: Too Much or Too Little

The tug between fear of disclosure and failure to disclose is a significant controversy if the public is to be protected. In effect, performance disclosures help to bridge the gap between traditional disclosures and those desired by many stakeholders. However, liability exposure, and the absence of auditing procedures and disclosure requirements for performance audit reports in the private sector, will continue to impede the proliferation of performance and accountability reporting. In the public sector, where standards are fairly well-developed, accountability reporting is widely enhancing traditional financial reports.

The Marriott case exemplifies a situation where there are questions of accountability. The original intent of management was both noble and ignoble. Noble was the aggressiveness and innovation in improving the financial performance of the entity amidst an economic recession and real estate recession. Ignoble was the shifting of the burden of improved profitability from shareholders to debt holders. At issue is how to distribute accountability to different constituent groups without compromising the integrity of management or the achievement of improved performance. Marriott management is beginning to see the positive effects of their plan on financial health; debt holders and brokers are still aggrieved.

THE PRACTICE OF PERFORMANCE AUDITING FOR ACCOUNTABILITY

The practice of performance auditing has been developed to be useful in assessing the achievement of objectives by management. Because standards are not as fully developed in performance audit as they are in financial audit, different practices have evolved in different contexts. However, some characteristics are common across applications. Below, the performance audit environment is discussed, followed by a discussion of how performance auditing relates to other types of audits. Then, engagement and scope factors are examined. Finally, the analytical constructs which underpin the practice of performance audit are presented.

Audit Theory Using Agency Theory

As agency theory has demonstrated in research, the distance between shareholders and managers imposes certain costs upon a firm. Because shareholders cannot directly observe management, they rely upon independent evidence that management is operating in shareholder's interests, and are willing to bear the cost of a financial audit to obtain this independent evidence. In this way, the cost of the audit is offset by its value in attracting and maintaining capital providers. These providers would not invest without confidence that resources and claims of the firm are reasonably accurate. Capital providers are free to withdraw from investments in the event of dissatisfaction because the capital marketplace provides many opportunities.

In the public sector, the system of taxation assures a stream of capital to governmental units, which do not, in any strict sense, have to compete for funds. Dissatisfaction with the operation of a municipal, state, or federal unit provides ample fodder for scandalous media reports, but a relatively inefficient and cumbersome process for withdrawl of funds by taxpayers. This said, it is clear that inefficiencies both exist and persist in governmental units because accountability is weak due to such distance between the agents (governmental managers) and the shareholders (taxpayers).

As competition becomes more intense in both the public and private sector for new capital, it is instructive to note that government has grown much more rapidly than the private sector. Tax rates have risen to foster more redistribution of income than ever before, but also government's widespread gobbling of capital to attack expensive modern dilemmas, such as improved healthcare, drug interdiction and treatment, gun control and registration, AIDS, boarder babies, the homeless, and low-cost availability of college education.

In developed nations, such as the United States, urban problems including drugs, poverty, violence, and joblessness absorb vast resources. In developing nations funds are desperately needed to improve infrastructure in goods and services such as transportation, education, healthcare, and communications systems. Hence, a methodology which will assist in the decision-making process of setting output goals and designating resources to meet those goals is a useful tool. Furthermore, in the wake of municipal bankruptcies, and bankruptcies of school systems in several urban areas, the realignment of allocation of tax revenues must take place in an efficient environment. That is, decisions must be made in which the reallocation of tax dollars are at least marginally effective for the uses to which they are put; and reallocation of state revenues to municipal governments will be closely monitored for waste or fraud. Performance auditing is a valuable tool, both for assessment of the need for scarce dollars, and the effectiveness of having supplied the funds for the common purposes. The specification of goals, resource inputs, and results can be both quantitative as well as qualitative. Reporting on results permits capital providers to apply pressure to capital users, even in the indirect environment of government.

There are, then, four major dimensions to the accountability function: *economy* in obtaining resources at least cost; *efficiency*, in finding the best use of resources; *effectiveness*, in maximizing the attainment of objectives; and *comprehensive reporting*, in communicating the accountability of management to the public in their utilization of resources, and in meeting policy goals. This is depicted in Figure 2.1.

The process of accountability conforms to three phases: a budget which applies resources to measurable outputs, the management process in which resources are used for the attainment of goals, and the evaluation phase in which outputs are assessed and results are reported. Included in the evaluation phase is the essential appraisal of corrections and any revisions which need to be made in the allocation of resources or in controls.

Budgets are built upon goals and objectives. Resources are allocated, then, in response to the need to achieve goals and objectives. The source of these resources may be either acquisition of new resources or redeployment of existing firm personnel and assets.

Management, with a clear understanding of objectives and goals, then has discretion to employment resources to fulfill the firm or public entities' strategic plan. Modern management constructs have demonstrated repeatedly that latitude given to managers results in innovation, positive morale, and enhanced performance. The explicit requirement of relating resources to goals aids managers in keeping their direction toward positive performance, while still providing them with flexibility and the ability to take risks.

The evaluation phase in the flow of the performance audit includes quantitative and qualitative measurements. A comparison of the resources used with the attainment

Figure 2.1
The Process of Performance Audit

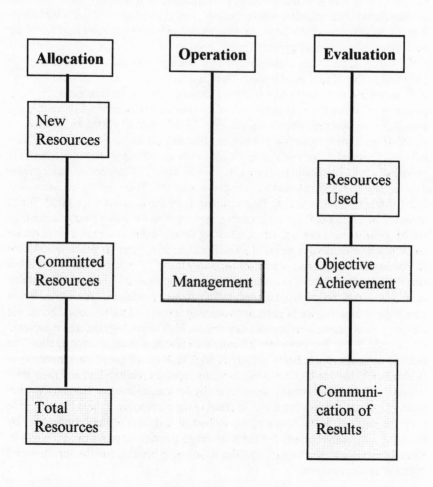

of goals provides an indication of performance. Results are reported; an analysis of corrective actions, redeployment of resources, and the extent to which goals have been realized is included in the report.

Private Financial Reporting Trends

In the private sector financial audits have been the primary mechanism to achieve accountability. But increasing controversy over the nature and amount of information disclosed in annual reports persists. Because of this, and because of the increasing complexity of financial transactions, a trend towards disclosing more "soft," or nonquantitative data, paired with the opposing trend of keeping sometimes significant financial liabilities off of the financial statements, has evolved. Some examples of the first trend, wherein management finds a need to better explain and predict their performance, include the rapidly expanding management discussion and analysis (MD&A) section of the annual report. There is a more minor but significant increase in firms willing to present projections and forward-looking information on financial performance in annual reports. Examples of the opposing trend, wherein management avoids or contracts their financial statement of liabilities, include the heavy increase in off-balance sheet financing techniques, debt defeasance, and opposition to fully booking financial obligations to employees such as retirement benefits other than pensions. The United States recently renegotiated with the Kingdom of Saudi Arabia their commitments to purchase U.S. defense equipment. This was needed because of Saudi Arabia's decline in cash flow resulting from the lowered price of oil. In an unusual move, major defense contractors joined together to form a partnership which would "hold" (i.e., "book") the debt, allowing Saudi Arabia to spread their purchase commitments over a longer period of time. Saudi Arabia agreed to guarantee the debt so that the partnership could acquire the necessary loans. The partnership, then, is left with the liabilities, while the contracting companies continue to show a positive stream of income and cash flow from the reduced equipment purchases. The United States wins because maintenance of defense contracting is essential for continued economic recovery; Saudi Arabia wins because they acquire high technology defense equipment at a rate which they can more easily handle until revenues from oil exports rise. The defense contractors win because there is no default on the purchase commitments (which would have to be written off, reducing reported profitability) and their sales remain steady; the partnership is made secure by the loan guarantee. But, on the other hand, one clearly motivating factor in creating the partnership to hold the debt, is to keep the debt off of the books of the individual divisions of the contractors. By financing off-balance sheet, the firms' leverage position appears more favorable. Thus, the contractors aim for capital market information benefits and the attraction and retention of shareholders.

Public Sector Financial Reporting Trends

In the public sector, the process is often the same, but results may be different. In the public and third (i.e., quasipublic) sector, monopoly benefits most often prevail, and there is not competition for capital in any strict sense. The efficient capital market mechanism releasing the flow of capital to the most efficient segment in the private sector does not operate in the public arena. In effect, waste and unreasonable risk by management does not cause capital flows to cease. Rather, laws and taxation policy are the source of capital allocation, and redistribution of funds from more wealthy to less wealthy school districts, municipalities, states, and even individuals is taken as a given. The balkiness of redirecting capital flows when waste, fraud, or ineffectiveness occurs in the public sector imposes different burdens upon managers in the quest for accountability. This is the case both in terms of collecting information and in terms of information reporting systems.

A further complication in the public sector relates to the issue of productivity measures. Every shareholder, creditor, and bondholder of a private firm is keenly interested in profitability. But citizens, as shareholders in public entities such as municipalities, states, and federal agencies, find it difficult to standardize information into a system which discloses performance in a meaningful way. Even when performance reporting takes place, public agency responsiveness to demands for better controls is slow and unwieldy. An example of this is easily found in the federal government. The initiation of inspector generals in federal agencies was expected to dramatically improve operational efficiency. When inspector generals' reports went largely unheeded, such as at Housing and Urban Development, government went further to try to gain better control. The Chief Financial Officer program, which has gone into effect for federal agencies, is another laudable and widespread effort to attain accountability in the federal bureaucracy. But implementation of recommendations for reforms rests within agencies which are often loathe to change. Thus, change is still slow in coming. The Yellow Book, used for performance auditing standards in federal applications is, however, far more developed than standards in the private sector. See Figure 2.2.

The framework for accountability, then, implies explicit development of performance standards and measurements to respond to the need for accountability. Internal control is a fundamental building block upon which to base a performance audit. Financial management controls, information, and reporting provide quantitative information in the understanding and exposure of accountability of an enterprise. The assessment of risk and the compilation of strategic plans and objectives help the entity to define and refine goals and deploy resources. Then, the evaluation of economy, efficiency, and effectiveness along with sustainability can be measured and reported upon for accountability.

Comprehensive Auditing

A thorough and practical mechanism to measure and report on performance takes place through a series of integrated audits. Each audit fulfills the objective of accountability by evaluating the relevant risk factors, existing internal controls, compliance evaluation, and a reporting function. While each audit has a distinct focus, there is necessarily some overlap between them. It is possible for an organization to perform each subaudit independently, with varying specifications for scope and attestation. Some audits may be eliminated, and different frequencies may be assigned to the various audits depending on the inherent riskiness of the organization or unit.

Figure 2.2
The Context of Performance Audit

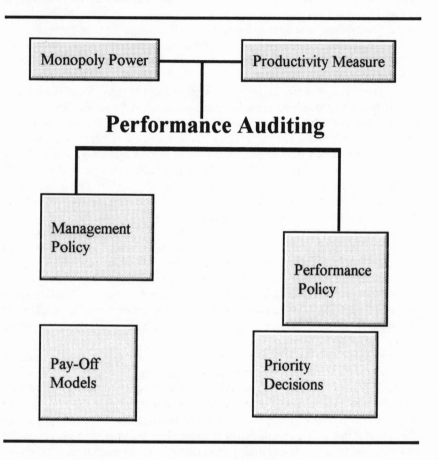

Nevertheless, the combination of the audits provides strong entity evaluation and has a synergistic effect on accountability. The combined audits provide an opportunity to comprehensively compare value-for-money in an organization, and reports on the oversight of management on the resources they control, as in Figure 2.3.

In general, any audit consists of a series of inquiries, tests, and reporting. Inquiries are made by interview, observation, and examination of substantive evidence in order to obtain an understanding of the client. Tests are performed to confirm or deny the understandings and assumptions which were made in the first phase. The last phase, reporting, provides information to interested parties on the results of the audit.[12]

The phases of an audit, then, are:

•   background investigation into the macroenvironment in which the client or entity exists, including the relevant economy, the industry, and the firm. In the public

Figure 2.3
Cumulative and Synergistic Effect of Audits

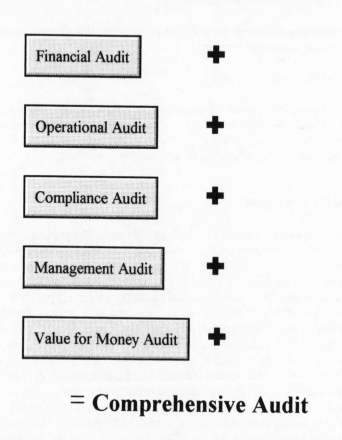

= **Comprehensive Audit**

sector, related factors would be the economy, the relevant federal, state, and local interrelationships, and the citizenship.

- obtaining substantive evidence of the environment, and synthesizing the relevant relationships.

- assessing riskiness of various activities of the entity in order to use audit time efficiently in testing documents and observations.

- investigating controls within the entity which operate to provide assurance that procedures and policies of the entity are working toward entity goals.

- testing transactions to verify substantive assumptions about the activities of the entity and tracing through relationships.

- documenting results of the audit; in many cases, this phase also reflects the expression of an audit opinion.

- providing a report on results.

While these various phases are adjusted according to budget, audit scope, audit budget, and audit objective, they provide a framework for the performance of various types of audits. The common types of audits are briefly described below in the context of contemporary events which beg for accountability reporting.

The Financial Audit

The most well-known audit is the *financial audit*. The primary function of the financial audit is to investigate and evaluate internal controls related to safeguarding entity assets, and to attest to whether the financial statements and accompanying notes on the statements are reasonably stated. In addition, an attestation addresses whether the financial statements conform to generally accepted accounting principles and fairly represent the entity's financial position. Evaluation of internal controls in the organization is the bedrock on which the financial audit rests. Outside auditors use the analysis of internal control in the organization to make audit decisions on scope, evidence, and the audit plan itself.

In addition to discouraging fraudulent financial reporting, the financial audit provides assurance to the capital market that financial management risk is adequately portrayed in the financial statements. This assurance makes shareholders, suppliers, and bankers willing to extend capital or credit. In the public sector, the signaling to citizens provides assurance that tax dollars are both needed and well-spent. In the case of state and local government, financial statements have improved in recent years, with the active participation of the Governmental Accounting Standards Board in promulgating financial reporting standards. Unfortunately, federal financial reporting is still not user-friendly, not well-coordinated, and not uniform. But improvements in this area are taking place with the innovation of the Chief Financial Officers Act as well as the initiation of a federal financial standards advisory board which deliberates on federal accounting standards.

Several actual cases will illustrate the utility of the financial audit; but first some cautionary notes should be presented. Financial audits do not eliminate the existence of financial fraud; to perform such an audit would be prohibitively expensive and yield a low benefit/cost relationship. Nor does the presence of a financial audit eliminate investment risk. Rather, the purpose is to make sure that the financial statements adequately portray the risk of the entity. In addition, it is easy to draw a distinction between *audit failure* and *business failure* and important to note that the two are entirely different. Audit failure occurs when audits do not perform their duties according to generally accepted auditing standards. Audit failure is relatively rare, but widely publicized when it occurs. Business failure occurs when a business is no longer a going concern, usually because liabilities are larger than the assets of the entity; while there are many reasons why businesses fail, ultimately bankruptcy involves negative cash flow and failure of the entity to have credit extended to it. This situation has pertained to both private corporations as well as several municipalities in recent years. While the federal government operates at a deficit, its credit worthiness has been upheld, and thus, it does not fail even in the face of negative cash flow.

Examples of Financial Audit

Let's look at some examples of problems which are in the domain of a financial audit. In a widespread scandal involving 83 individuals, a former chairman of the Japanese telephone company, Nippon Telegraph and Telephone (NT&T), stood accused of bribery for receiving undervalued stock as a bribe. Mr. Shinto pleaded not guilty, saying he accepted the unlisted stock which yielded him a quick $150,000 profit, but felt it was not a bribe.[13] Today there are many required disclosures for key directors and executives of private firms. Mr. Shinto was the individual responsible for taking NT&T private from the public sector. The bribe accusation originates from his potential usefulness in the company whose stock he received to receive telecommunications contracts.

This is an interesting case, because it involves financial misdeeds. However, it would be extraordinarily difficult for a financial audit of NT&T to uncover them because it involves the personal finances of the chairman. On the other hand, an audit of Recruit, the company whose stock was transferred to Mr. Shinto, would likely uncover the irregularities. This, then, is a good example of an ambiguous situation which involves financial controls, but needs the assurance of the universality of the United States' system, that publicly-held companies receive audits. This systemic audit policy inherently strengthens each individual audit as interrelationships are examined at different times by different auditors in the bulk of U.S. businesses.

In another interesting example, a parent company, Texas Air, was accused of financially cannibalizing one of its subsidiaries, Eastern Air Lines, to favor another, Continental. Lest the term "financial cannibalizing" disturb the reader, it may be noted that an Air Line Pilots Association attorney referred to the financial misdealing as "rape."[14] In fact, the allegations include evidence that Texas Air's purchase of Eastern Airlines was not intended to keep Eastern as a going concern, but to improve the financial positions of the parent and subsidiary, Continental. In one transaction, the computerized ticketing system of Eastern was sold to Texas Air for $100 million, who then sold *half* of the same system to a General Motors subsidiary for $250 million.[15] A financial audit of the parent would uncover the intercorporate sale transaction, which would be eliminated upon consolidation for financial reporting purposes.

Similarly, the significant profit from the sale to an outside entity would be evaluated in a financial audit. Even though a financial audit would cover the consolidated entity, the intercorporate sale would be relevant, and a financial audit would examine the transaction because of its materiality. This case was settled by the parent company "reimbursing" the subsidiary $280 million to avoid legal proceedings.

A case in the public sector also illustrates the domain of the financial audit. The District of Columbia, still reeling from the conviction of its mayor for possession and use of illegal drugs, also suffered the embarrassment of allegations of influence peddling between a major city contractor, John Clyburn, and city administrator Elijah Rivers. The D.C. Auditor found improper awarding of a contract for drug counseling to a Clyburn firm, DISC, and found evidence that Rivers had taken responsibility to make sure that DISC received the contract, even allowing DISC to design the contract.[16] In a financial audit of the city's books the audit uncovered irregularities when an FBI audit was also taking place. This is an example of the significance of internal controls in the public sector and the effectiveness of sampling transactions to make sure that the internal control policies exist. Just as important, the audit makes sure that the policies are being followed.

Financial audits do not eliminate fraud but rather assess the risk of fraud and report on controls which curtail fraud. Auditors are under siege for situations in which fraud has been found, undetected by auditors.

The Operational Audit

An *operational audit* enhances the financial audit. An operational audit looks more broadly at operational systems in the organization, including recruiting and hiring systems, procurement systems, job order systems, product costing systems, and others. Like the financial audit, internal control policies and practices are critical to evaluate. This is because observance and verification of all of the steps in an operating system would be prohibitively expensive. Therefore, the existence of internal control policies and procedures is the building block upon which the audit proceeds. The audit may then be designed to test the reliability of the system.

The distinction between the operational audit and the financial audit pertains to the scope of the systems audited. In the financial audit the primary focus will be the financial recording and reporting system, and the operational systems which deal with safeguarding assets. In the operational audit in-depth reviews of costing and pricing systems may be of primary interest, or alternatively, the systems dealing with product delivery or customer satisfaction. While in the long run it is clear that all operating systems in the entity affect profitability and financial position, not all operating systems are critical to the financial audit objective of providing assurance that the financial statements reasonably reflect the financial position of the firm. Operational audits lead to improvements in efficiency, effectiveness, and economy by discovering weaknesses in policy or procedure, or by bringing out failures in the application of policy or procedure. In order to perform an operational audit many specialists beyond accounting experts must be involved.

The Compliance Audit

Compliance audits are receiving more attention in recent years as part of the audit process. Compliance audits evaluate whether an entity is adhering to all relevant rules, regulations, laws, and standards which pertain to the entity. Examples of areas which are of concern to most enterprises are minimum wage laws, environmental laws, codes of ethics pertaining to professionals, health codes, fire codes, pension plan requirements (including eligibility, record-keeping, qualifying the plan, etc.). While many compliance audits address upholding laws, they are not limited to the private sector. Many state, local, and federal entities use compliance audits, and formal standards mandate their use.

Consider, for example, the Department of Health and Human Services. They must qualify individuals for social services plans such as food stamps, housing vouchers, and medical care. They must similarly qualify providers of services. Thus, they are involved in controlling both recipients and providers of services. Because there are so many service providers, businesses, and government agencies involved, as well as the myriad of largely uncoordinated rules and regulations of many government agencies, a compliance audit is both complex and costly. Therefore, most organizations will perform a preaudit risk analysis; this will identify target areas for the audit.

Compliance audits, in particular, suggest many sinkholes for auditors. In most cases auditors will find that the organization employs policies instructing managers and other personnel to adhere to relevant laws. In addition, it would be rare to encounter an organization which did not formalize and disseminate procedures for personnel to follow to ensure adherence to regulations. But, especially in the case of compliance audits, direct evidence of adherence may be difficult to obtain, leaving an auditor to review internal controls (policy, procedures, monitoring), and to back up this review with interviews and some observations of management. In recent years, it has proved to be particularly perilous to rely on management assertions. In the majority of cases where management has not reported accurately they did not set out to deceive the auditor, but made assumptions or painted too rosy a picture of events. In some cases upper managers have relied upon lower level managers who have masked events to avoid responsibility for errors in judgment or in fact.

The reporting of environmental matters in particular poses significant problems for managers and their auditors. The FASB recently issued a consensus memorandum on reporting and valuing environmental liabilities.[17] Valuation issues are also affected by the accounting and reporting of loss contingencies, which address potential claims.[18] These professional guidelines instruct companies to promptly disclose and book potential claims, rather than waiting for events to occur which may assist in making a better estimate of claims. This is a conservative approach, i.e., making a reasonable estimate and disclosing is deemed preferable to making a more accurate estimate with delay until sufficient data is available to assess the claim. Conservatism is consistent with the spirit of timely disclosure of risk. The professional literature suggests that managers and their auditors evaluate environmental liabilities by examining and explicitly listing whether they are potentially responsible parties

(PRPs) as defined by the Environmental Protection Agency. Sometimes multiple PRPs exist and may be jointly and severally liable for damage or clean-up. Auditors are increasingly including narrative analysis in the audit report to supplement the footnote financial disclosures on contingencies related to environmental costs. To illustrate the complexity of environmental compliance and business or government exposure to environmental risks, auditors may search for evidence by asking management about conditions such as:

- compliance with state, local, and federal environmental laws

- ownership of subsidiaries which are environmentally at risk

- production or inventories which are environmentally at risk

- land use, land acquisitions, and land transactions (particularly bargain purchases of land which may be indicative of land which has environmental hazards)

- acquisition, use, or production of chemicals

- inspection policies and records

- maintenance of a record of applicable environmental laws

- procedures for becoming aware of relevant new environmental laws

- certifications from authorities for environmental compliance

In all, a compliance audit assesses the degree to which the entity abides by pertinent rules, regulations, standards, and laws. This concept has expanded in recent years to include exposure, risk, and potential claims against the entity on these matters by the promulgation and enhanced interpretation of contingency claims.

The Management Audit

Management audit is an amorphous term usually referring to the effectiveness of management in meeting strategic goals, in planning, and in controlling. At the present time most management audits are performed by management themselves, or management consultants, rather than internal or external auditors. Also, the reporting mechanisms for management audits are not standardized, leading to difficulty in public comprehension. This also impedes any ability to compare managements of different entities. However, the focus on management effectiveness is critical in the survival and competitiveness of the organization. As formal standards evolve, capital market efficiency will be significantly enhanced by public responsiveness to disclosures on management effectiveness.

The overwhelming interest in health care cost containment provides an interesting example of management audit. Hospitals in the District of Columbia, whether public or private, are required to provide services regardless of ability to pay. This requirement has led several urban university teaching hospitals to suffer inordinately high losses for which there is no compensation. The financial stress placed upon the hospitals and their parent universities has led to efforts toward cost containment to be even more critical than in other municipalities. At Georgetown University Hospital, management undertook the usual steps to regain financial health: more out patient surgery, limited hospital stays, increased efforts at collecting fees. But in a strategic management self-audit, surprising and more unusual tactics were discovered. At the suggestion of employees, $30,000 per year is being saved by eliminating the plastic wrapping on clean sheets; by using unbleached paper towels instead of white ones, nearly $15,000 per year is saved. And by not dusting baby powder on just-bathed patients, $8,000 per year in costs are eradicated.[19] These changes which abolish costs without any impact on patient health, safety, or comfort, resulted from management self-examination of policies, procedures, and purchasing plans which did not contribute to the overall goals of providing quality services to patients.

A more sinister example of the potential benefit of management audits involves the public sector. In New York State, the legislature has never enacted a law which prohibits misuse of funds. While a financial audit would be expected to find such fraud, it was a management audit which exposed a State Senator who had padded his payroll with no fewer than forty fictitious workers who did no work for the State, but did occasional work on the Senator's political campaigns.[20] Given the absence of a State law, only those workers who neither worked for the State, nor worked on political campaigns, were considered to be worth prosecuting. The Appellate Division found that Senators could, under the current laws, use State funds to pay employees to mow their lawns and not be prosecuted. A State Supreme Court Justice noted that it was up to the voters to force the issue into legislation. A routine audit which related all activities or all expenditures to state goals would clearly identify the paid employees without jobs to be without merit. The most basic accountability appears to be missing in this case.

In a management audit, focus is directed toward:

- risk analysis: areas where management has "exposure"

- strategic planning: policies and procedures used by management to insure that long-range plans are made and adherence is insured; setting goals

- flexibility; ability to respond in an appropriate and timely manner to situations which threaten achievement of goals

- traditional measures of efficiency, effectiveness, and economy: achievement of goals at least cost, using scarce resources appropriately

- measurement and reporting of achievements: disseminating the management information to capital market participants to enhance equity valuation in a private firm, or to enhance public support in the public sector

• mechanisms for feedback and responses: post-goal evaluation, adjustment, and articulation of goal amendments.

In almost every situation conflicts of interest arise, which make the management audit just as valuable as the financial audit. Consider an example of a situation which would not have shown up in a financial audit, but which would be discovered with the presence of a formal management audit. It involves scientific researchers who maintain equity positions in the drug firms for which they work.[21] A bitter dispute arose between stockholders and a scientist who sold his own stock when he discovered that the eye medication he was developing for the company was ineffective. In the case, the scientist, affiliated with Harvard Medical School and the Massachusetts Eye and Ear Infirmary, was judged by these institutions to have misled the company about his results on the medication trials, and to have a conflict of interest caused by his ownership of equity in the company. On the other hand, it was legal for the researcher to purchase the stock. The issue is whether researchers who place themselves in these circumstances willfully manipulate the stock prices by reporting the promise of an innovative new discovery, then sell the stock as it reflects the potential new market, gaining profits in the process. The National Institutes of Health, for example, does not permit its own researchers to purchase equity interests in drug companies whose work overlaps that of the researcher.[22] And some publications, such as the prestigious *New England Journal of Medicine* have policies requiring scientific authors to disclose equity interests in footnotes or elsewhere in the publication. Congressional hearings have thus far failed to resolve the ethical issue.

Given the media, Congressional, and scientific community attention to this matter, a management audit would be expected to flag it as a risk area. As a designated risk area policies, procedures, internal controls, and reporting mechanisms would be implemented. Then, the audit itself would assess and report on adherence with the entity's relevant standards. In this way, the management audit provides supplemental assurance to the financial audit regarding the entity's management.

Other areas addressed by the management audit are determined by a risk analysis which details the areas of significant interest to stakeholders in the entity. Some examples include:

• background checks and previous experience of management

• management compensation and performance issues

• management's adherence to long-range goals

• management's success in strategic planning

• management's ability to react and respond to need for change

- depth and breadth of management expertise and appropriateness of allocation of management across functional areas.

Management audits are appropriately conducted in conjunction with other organizational initiatives such as Total Quality Management, reengineering, or management by objectives. Use of outside consultants is often most effective in evaluating management; however, much of the groundwork can be accomplished internally, using either an enhanced internal audit staff, or management itself.

The Value-for-money Audit

The *value-for-money audit* specifically addresses the concerns of economy, efficiency, and effectiveness, sometimes including stability and concerns. Value-for-money considerations emphasize achieving entity goals at least cost, with the most appropriate allocation of resources, while attaining stated objectives. Value-for-money audits are primarily done in the public sector at the current time and are being extended into more organizations as formalization of audit standards continues to evolve. These audits have been discussed previously and provide a highly useful adjunct to the traditional financial audit. For example, a financial audit may serve to ensure that money expended by the entity went towards the entity's payroll, and not by fraud to someone who is not an employee. But the financial audit does not assess whether the employee who was paid achieved the performance goals set out by the organization, or whether the employee's job is necessary. These dimensions are addressed by the particular audit which emphasized economy, efficiency, and effectiveness or value-for-money.

The Comprehensive Audit

When combined, the full range of audits, including audit reports, is designated as a *comprehensive audit*. The comprehensive audit, expansive in scope, and fulfilling multiple purposes, provides a thorough review of operations in such a way that stakeholders receive relevant information regarding performance. This audit does not attempt to review every facet of every operation in the organization.

Rather, through risk analysis, review of internal controls, and strategy, it allocates audit resources toward those areas which will provide the best cost/benefit coverage. In auditing and reporting on these areas, opportunities for improvements and assurance that the entity is "in control" are disclosed. Thus, stakeholders and capital markets are able to more appropriately place a valuation on the entity. Reporting is both positive and negative. Where negative findings occur as needs exist for improvements, these are noted. However, and equally significant, the positive reporting mechanism also generates constructive confidence that the organization is well-run. This assurance improves the competitive position of the firm. Thus, the audit expenditures are expected to be "returned" by the enhanced reputation the firm gains when assurance is given to outside parties that the entity is performing competitively on multiple dimensions, with particular emphasis on economy, efficiency, and effectiveness of operations.

ANALYTICAL CONCEPTS FOR PERFORMANCE AUDITING

The underlying analytical concepts of performance audit are multidisciplinary and rest on the foundations of general standards of auditing. Certainly, the two most basic concepts are independence and sufficient professional background of personnel engaged in the performance audit. Two subsidiary concepts are adequate authority and sufficient evidentiary matter. The procedural and reporting concepts of performance audit are discussed in chapter 3. In this section independence is discussed first, followed by consideration of training and background of the audit personnel. Then assessment of authority and access of audit personnel to substantive audit evidence is examined.

Independence

Independence is certainly the most crucial of the requirements for auditors in the performance of performance auditing. Because many audit staff people are employed by the public sector to audit public sector entities, these people should be external to the unit being audited, and have no vested interest in the outcome of the audit. This is less of a problem in the private sector. In the private sector and in some public sector environments external auditors are called in to execute performance audits. These external auditors should not have performed other services for the entity, such as strategic planning or management advisory services, because of the possibility of becoming involved in auditing one's own input into the system. It is not in good form to audit your own work. Part of the independence concept rests upon the ability of the auditor to carry out the audit; the scope of evidence and reporting must be determined by the audit team and not by management. If interference or limitations occur in scope, evidence, and reporting, the performance audit team cannot fulfill their audit mission and should withdraw from the engagement. Furthermore, while there are no professional standards in this area at this time a change in the audit team should be reported, especially if there are disagreements over scope, evidence, and reporting. Because of the diversity of audit standards now in existence for performance auditing extreme caution with regard to the independence of the auditor must be exercised.

Professional Expertise

Sufficient background of audit team managers and members must be maintained. Because of the diverse requirements of performance audit evaluation and evidence, the team is usually multidisciplinary and careful communication between team members must be stressed throughout all phases of the audit. Furthermore, nonaccountant specialists are frequently necessary as part of the audit team to provide subject area expertise that the auditors may lack or industry specialization knowledge. Background of audit team members will usually entail formal education as well as performance audit experience. The audit team which is engaged in the performance audit will most likely be considerably more experienced, on balance, and have more varied subject area specialization than the in-depth audit specialization of financial audit teams. While financial audit teams possess considerable industry specialization, most members hold auditing as their primary field of expertise. However, on the performance audit, many members will not be accounting or auditing experts. This fact has made the implementation of performance auditing more difficult, since the background requirements of the audit team may change drastically with the definition of the performance audit target. The fluidity of personnel background requirements makes it difficult to train team members; if it is possible to train them, the costs are high, since they may have to be retrained for the next engagement. This is why it is imperative for the private sector to be prepared to serve on performance audit engagements; by engaging external staff for a specific purpose, and a specific time frame, the audit target receives the best area specialists. Costs may be minimized to the audit target, then, since retraining is not necessary; by using flexible personnel allocation rather than engagement-specific training, and by allowing a performance auditor to develop in-depth subject area specialization, start-up costs and time are minimized.

Audit Authority and Access to Evidence

Performance auditors must have adequate authority to plan, implement, access and assess evidence, and report on their performance audit task. This authority may be legislated by statute or may be given by top management, regulators, or a board of directors. In any case, the auditors, within the scope of the audit, must be empowered to collect and analyze data and must have complete knowledge of their accountability function. Formal authority provides the auditor with the ability to collect evidence and ensures adequate cooperation from the audit target. Without formal and clearly defined authority the audit team will encounter roadblocks in its attempts to obtain and document substantive evidence. Also, because of the more fluid task of the performance audit, compared to a financial audit, more qualitative and less quantitative evidence is required; this may entail a considerable time commitment from the audit target for background information. Therefore, where statutory authority for the performance audit does not exist, the engagement letter should meticulously document the scope of the audit.

NOTES

1. For a complete discussion of the basic technique, see D. R. Sheldon and E. F. McNamara. *Value for Money Auditing in the Public Sector: Strategies for Accountability in*

the 1990's. IIA Monograph Series. Altamonte Springs, FL: The Institute of Internal Auditors. 1991.

2. For example, Owen, Mandel, Bradshaw, and Percy-Smith have worked in this area. David Owen. *Green Reporting: Accountancy and the Challenge of the Nineties*. London: Chapman & Hall. 1992; E. Mandel. "In Defense of Socialist Planning." *New Left Review* 159 (1986); J. Bradshaw. "The Concept of Need," *New Society* 30 (1972); J. Percy-Smith. "Auditing Social Needs: An Alternative Means of Evaluating Policy." *Seminar on Social Audit*. 1990.

3. The concept of social audit is discussed extensively in A. Belkaoui. *Socio-economic Accounting*. Westport, CT: Greenwood Press. 1984.

4. While the agency theory literature is extensive, see in particular, Wanda A. Wallace. "The Economic Role of the Audit in Free and Regulated Markets: A Review." *Research in Accounting Regulation*. Greenwich, CT: JAI Press. 1987.

5. Refer to F. Pomeranz, *The Successful Audit: New Ways to Reduce Risk Exposure and Increase Efficiency*. Homewood, IL: Business One Irwin. 1992.

6. A fine discussion of the role of information and accountability on neoclassical economics is found in Chapter 1 of C. R. Lehman. *Accounting's Changing Role in Social Conflict*. New York: Markus Wiener, Inc. 1992.

7. Regina E. Herzlinger and Denise Nitterhouse. *Financial Accounting and Managerial Control for Nonprofit Organizations*. Cincinnati: South-Western Publishing Co. 1994. p. 250.

8. Herzlinger and Nitterhouse. 1994. 250.

9. "Two Marriott's Better than One." *Wall Street Journal*. November 10, 1991, A:25:1.

10. Robert Stowe England. "Are Two Marriotts Better than One?" *Financial World* 16:22 (November 10, 1992): 28-29.

11. *Deloitte & Touche Review*. Special Supplement. March 22, 1993, p. 2.

12. One recent work addresses the accountability and efficiency of traditional audits and suggests adoption of additional concepts in the traditional auditing model to adapt to technology and other pressures. Felix Pomerantz. *The Successful Audit: New Ways to Reduce Risk Exposure and Increase Efficiency*. Homewood, IL: Business One Irwin. 1992.

13. "Tokyo Executive Pleads Not Guilty in Recruit Bribery Case." *New York Times* December 14, 1989, A:19:1.

14. "Texas Air Blamed in 12 Eastern Deals." *The Washington Post* March 2, 1990, F:1:4.

15. Ibid.

16. "Clyburn: Man to Know in D.C." *The Washington Post* May 5, 1989, A:1:1.

17. Financial Accounting Standards Board, *EITF Consensus 93-5. Accounting for Environmental Liabilities*. 1993.

18. SAB 92. *Accounting and Disclosures Relating to Loss Contingencies*. 1994.

19. "Layoffs Help D.C. Hospitals' Bottom Line, but Patient Advocates Warn on Uninsured." *The Washington Post* November 6, 1992, C:9.

20. "Flabby Logic on 'No-Shows'." *The New York Times* December 29, 1989, A:34:1.

21. Marilyn Chase. "Bad Chemistry: Mixing Science, Stocks, Raises Question of Bias in the Testing of Drugs." *The Wall Street Journal* January 26, 1989, A:1:1.

22. Chase. *The Wall Street Journal*. 1989.

Chapter 3

Making Performance Audits Work for You: Implementing the Performance Audit

INTRODUCTION

Audit quality means auditing the right things and auditing the things right.[1] While the preceding discussion has focused on auditing the right things it is time now to turn to the issue of auditing the things right. This chapter will be useful to those who are preparing to initiate, or want to know how to perform, a performance audit. The procedure is equally useful in both the private, and the public sector. The general approach is to plan the audit, obtain evidentiary matter, assess the evidence, and report on the audit. In order to perform the audit itself, standards of conduct apply (general standards), examination standards apply (performance standards), and reporting standards apply (accountability standards). As discussed in chapter 2, the context, the scope, and the analytical process must be carefully reviewed prior to the implementation of the performance audit. In this chapter, the following elements of the performance audit are examined in turn:

- the audit plan: pre-audit planning; audit engagement development

- the documentation of the audit program

- the audit evidence

- assessment, evaluation, and methodology

- reporting and accountability functions

This presentation is general by necessity, since the actual performance will depend upon the situation-specific engagement. But the full framework is provided to guide the implementation of the performance audit in any organizational unit. Then standards for the performance audit are discussed, especially with reference to formally promulgated professional standards. The three sets of standards addressed are:

- general standards

- examination standards

- reporting standards[2]

However, a significant difference between traditional financial audit and the performance audit is that the latter is forward-looking in nature, and material evidence may not be documented.[3]

Internal Control

A recurring theme in the performance concept is that effective control requires strong internal controls. However, the development, implementation, and monitoring of internal controls, while highly significant, is only a portion of the real significance of performance assessment of economy, efficiency, and effectiveness. In fact, value-for-money requires specifying resource allocation criteria which provides management with the appropriate resources to do the job, allowing them sufficient *flexibility* to do the job, and then holding them accountable for the use of the resources. This entails walking a fine line between developing strong internal control and permitting managerial flexibility.

This enables management, on a sometimes ad hoc basis, to reconfigure the allocation based on revised needs, external pressures, and dynamic policy objectives. If internal control conveyed the entire issue of value-for-money, performance auditing and operational auditing would not be two distinct functions in the assessment of management. Rather, performance auditing is required because a significant issue of accountability is managements' responsiveness, ability to predict market changes, innovativeness, and manpower planning appropriateness. Therefore, the risk analysis, which searches for areas where the performance benefit/cost relationship will remain significantly positive, is a critical part of the performance concept, and an important part of the performance audit planning. Internal controls should remain reasonably flexible to allow management to perform effectively; the performance audit then holds management accountable for its decisions and ultimate transformation of inputs into achievement of policy objectives.

Some Practice History

The demand for performance reporting and comprehensive audits to assure value-for-money is well-seasoned. In 1907, in Great Britain, the Departmental Committee on Accounts reported,[4]

It is generally agreed that as wide publicity as practicable should be given to the accounts of local authorities and that they should be published in such a form as to be intelligible to ratepayers possessed of average ability but without special knowledge of accountancy.

However, the practice and standards for performance auditing did not develop, and nearly seventy years later in Great Britain, the Layfield Committee was drawn to conclude that[5]

We believe that there is an obligation on local authorities to devise a means of providing the electorate with financial information about services in reasonably simple and straightforward terms.

An Example

For many years, comparisons between actual expenditures and budgets, on a line item basis, have been the standard by which financial management has been assessed in the private sector. In accordance with the quotes above, it is intelligible, reasonably simple, and straightforward. The problem with this is made clear by reference to a recent example in the State of Maryland. The State initiated a public lottery which made the previously outlawed gambling statutes obsolete. The new state lottery was the only form of legal numbers gambling available after more than thirty years' abstinence due to its legislated illegality. The purpose of the state lottery was to generate revenues and therefore enhance public treasuries. Consistent with the budget, revenues were generated, and the variance between budget and revenue was insignificant. However, the state not long after decided to provide a public program for compulsive gamblers. This program provided intensive counseling and other outpatient services. The program achieved adherence to the budget, and therefore, budget and actual expenditure comparison generated no significant variance. Now, individually, the programs were both successful, as well as well-managed; revenues and expenditures for each program were in balance and within budgeted amounts. But a significant analysis was clearly missing. The more relevant and significant analysis reveals two things: first, the revenue from the lottery was much less attractive when the compulsive gambler public rehabilitation program cost was subtracted. Second, lotteries have been found to *replace*, not *enhance* public funds. The lottery actually functions as an extremely regressive, but voluntary, tax. The significant analysis needed to perform this assessment is, of course, the performance audit, which evaluates the programs' interrelationships, as well as measuring the extent to which the individual programs meet objectives. The performance audit would also contain considerations of *effectiveness:* are there more effective ways to generate revenues?

THE AUDIT PLAN

The audit plan really consists of at least three stages: the pre-audit plan, the planning of the audit engagement, and the documentation of the audit program.

Pre-Audit Planning

Pre-audit planning involves taking a hard look at the organizational units and determining where to put the audit resources. Many people refer to this evaluation as a *"risk analysis"* phase; this is the stage where the auditors who are charged with managing the performance task interview management, begin to gain a knowledge of the purpose and operational goals of the unit, and begin to try to understand the operation of the unit. The risk analysis has, as its purpose, the assessment of the probable areas where the performance of the performance audit would yield the greatest results.

The risk referred to above entails looking at areas of management, or areas of operations, or a particular phase of an operation; by reviewing the complexity, the internal control procedures, and the materiality of the resources used in the unit, the auditor begins to gain an appreciation for the benefit/cost payoffs. The higher the benefit/cost payoff, the higher the ranking for the performance of a performance audit, all other factors being held constant. As the ranking of audit targets unfolds, audit management generates a list, in a hierarchy, of audit priorities. Furthermore, through this ranking process audit management initiates a basic understanding of the purposes and operations of the unit being investigated. This initial understanding is crucial for the compilation of resources needed to perform the audit.

The performance audit is distinct from financial and compliance audits in the extremely wide range of audit specialists and subject matter specialists it requires. In addition to the traditional auditor, the auditor specifically schooled in the process and techniques of performance audit needs to be engaged. Also, economists, statisticians, and other support personnel are often needed. Furthermore, area experts in the audit target (teachers for schools, hospital administrators in the health area, production managers in the manufacturing setting, mounted police in the enforcement area) must be designated.

Audit Plan Development

Subsequent to the pre-audit planning phase, in which the risk assessment is performed, the audit plan can begin to be pulled together. The detailed audit plan itself is drawn up. Then the timetable for performance of the audit, the personnel requirements and selection, and the budgeted cost can be configured.

In order to proceed with the audit plan the audit management must become familiar with the environment in which they will examine evidence and must gain introductory expertise in the application of the business unit which is the audit target. This background environmental analysis is depicted in Figure 3.1. Several steps are executed in turn, for the development of the audit plan. Use of the plan is usually situation specific.

Background Analysis

First, audit management should obtain some of the background of the audit target and should delve into the history of the evolution of that unit. Management itself should be integrated into the collection of data. This enables the audit team to form a relevant perspective on how the business unit fits into the general purpose of the overall enterprise. Second, the audit team needs to obtain the basic and formal corporate culture of the organization; this is typically represented by any relevant code of conduct or code of ethics to which the business unit subscribes. In some applications this is supplemented by other additional correspondence between the top management and other personnel. Any policy statements which have broad applicability should be obtained and studied for relevance to the audit plan. Third, the audit management will want to examine, in some detail, the internal audit controls, and will interview the internal audit staff. The internal control will, as in the other audits, affect the scope of the audit, and the magnitude and type of audit evidence which must be obtained. Fourth, some comparative analyses will be useful and sometimes critical to the compilation of the audit plan. Comparative analysis of similar units within the organization will be useful, if they are available for study. In any event, industry comparison in the private sector, or other federal, state, local, or municipal offices with similar characteristics should be examined. This comparative analysis provides the range of acceptability or breadth of operational expectations upon which the audit management may want to depend for scope and evidentiary matter. Firm specific data is also useful, for general background information, for control purposes, for comparability of input/output relationships, and for expectations of operational similarity.

After the industry and agency-specific data is compiled, it is incumbent on the audit management team to become familiar with the organizational unit. Their expectations have already been formed in a preliminary way by the foregoing investigation. Now the team will obtain introductory information from the financial audit, the compliance audit, the operational audit, and the management audit; the depth will depend on the number of these audits which have been performed.

Finally, the audit team will attempt to assess the potential impact of the environmental factors on the scope and evidentiary matter, and will document and internalize the accountability relationships. The accountability relationships describe the link between the audit target, the performance audit team, and the constituent groups who have an interest in the performance audit report and a right to access the performance audit report.

In some applications confidentiality of the report is maintained and the accountability in the performance audit report is to management itself. In others the audit report is public and the accountability is to the legislature.

Timetable

A timetable for execution of the audit can be prepared at this point. The audit program depicts the scope, the evidence, the methodology which will be used. The accountability relationships will have been designated for reporting purposes.

Figure 3.1
Audit Plan Development

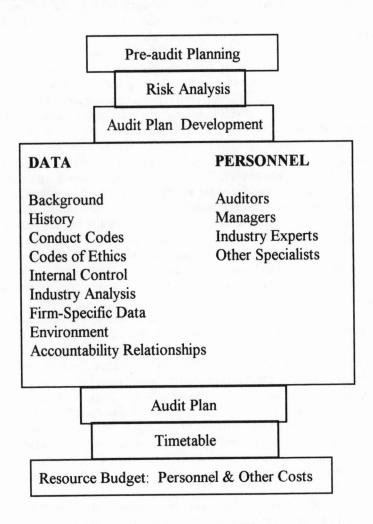

The personnel needs have been identified. The mechanisms for establishing input/output measurements and benefit/cost predictions have been developed. The timetable can take many forms, but as a basic tool a simple chart can be produced, which lists:

- the steps which need to be performed to implement the audit

- the resources which will be allocated to each step

- the approximate time budgeted for the execution of the audit steps

The timetable should be developed in cooperation with the personnel assigned to the audit, as well as the management of the business unit; this recommendation is a straightforward application of the widely recognized observation that the ability of employees to assist in the development of standards has the effect of strengthening their support for acceptance of the standards.

Since the audit function is labor intensive, two factors converge in determining staffing; the depth of experience needed and the breadth of expertise needed combine to determine the major portion of the audit cost. The assessment of personnel needs for the audit is often performed in the pre-audit planning stage of the performance audit. A plan for the acquisition of personnel services must be prepared at the point when the audit management has sufficient knowledge to develop a listing of employee needs. Four factors will affect the selection of the audit staff team:

- audit program need

- expertise

- experience

- availability

These are presented in Figure 3.2.

Cost and Resource Development

The cost for the performance audit is dependent upon the resource decisions made in the audit plan, which is, in turn, dependent upon the scope of the audit. There are two types of "costs" which need to be considered for an appropriate benefit/cost evaluation. First are the explicit costs of performing the audit itself. These costs include personnel cost for the audit staff, and other directly attributed costs such as support personnel for word processing, computer use, supplies, telephone, and fax. These costs also include indirect costs of running the performance audit which are explicit costs; for example, consider audit supervisory personnel, allocations from the internal audit staff assigned to the project, and overhead allocation from the performance audit administrative offices. The explicit costs can be pulled together, documented for budgeting purposes, identified as fixed or variable, direct or indirect, and totaled.

Figure 3.2
Audit Staffing

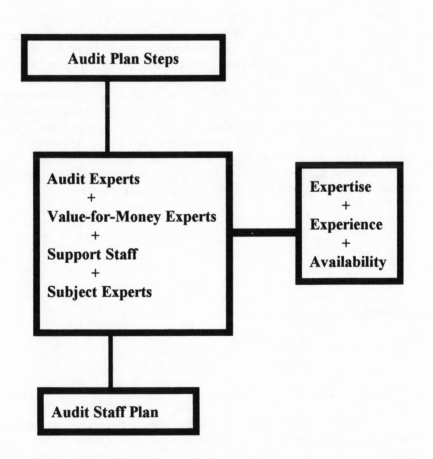

Considering Opportunity Cost

However, there is another type of cost to consider in developing the expected benefit/cost ratio. These are the opportunity costs in absorbing the time of management and other personnel in the operating unit which is the audit target. These costs are extremely difficult to control and predict because they may remain largely unknown until the audit is actually underway. They depend upon the attitude and experience of management and other operating personnel in dealing with auditors, and often upon the sensitivity of the audit team in eliciting information in a nonthreatening context. The opportunity costs may be significant and may take management away from critical functions; even more significant is the fact that management may be reluctant to be innovative and may stifle creativity because of the difficultly in defending unorthodox practices to the audit team. The best way to handle these complications is to structure internal controls to be sufficiently flexible to let management take risks, document and control the resources allocated to them, and hold this management responsible for the outcome. Under any application of performance audit some recognition should be given to the opportunity costs of using management and operating personnel time for the appropriate performance of performance audit. This is important both for the relevant recognition of costs as well as for managing the audit effectively.

THE AUDIT PROGRAM

The audit program itself should proceed along the time/cost/event chart that was examined above. In order to control and manage the audit actual progress should be tracked in the three areas (time, cost, event) and compared with the audit plan. Because the performance audit focuses on forward-looking information and often uses "soft" nonfinancial data, this type of audit is, by its very nature, complex and difficult to design. Furthermore, there tends to be considerable overlapping of documentation, background information, and audit evidence. However, the reliance upon component audits lessens the burden. In Figure 3.3 the conceptual differences between the component audit purposes which will be used in the performance audit are presented.

Implementation

In the implementation of the audit plan, the program must have the tacit approval of management. As has been mentioned, the solicitation of management's input and support will not only enhance the audit plan and evidentiary matter, but will make the audit program run more smoothly. In the public sector, the audit team should either have statutory authority or clearly defined objectives from the inspector general's office. In the private sector, support and guidance, as well as authority, should be obtained from the board of directors and from the board's audit committee. These authoritative officers should, along with management, work with the performance

Figure 3.3
Components of Comprehensive Audit

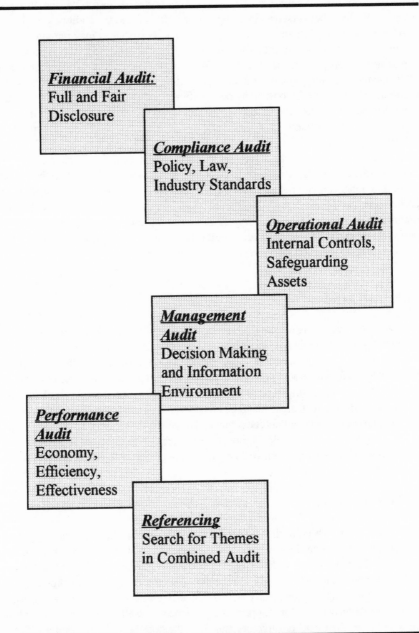

audit team. A consultatory style throughout the performance audit is recommended.

A primary function of the performance audit is the examination of internal controls, including recommendations for internal control improvements. But the difference between the performance audit internal control investigations and the internal control review performed in the operational audit is significant. In the performance audit, the focus is broad, the scope is wider, the interrelationships are more important, and the internal controls are linked in concrete ways to effectiveness, economy, and efficiency. That is, in the performance audit, the operational audit acts as basic input data. The performance audit adds the dimension of measurement of the operational impact of internal controls on economy, efficiency, and effectiveness.

Inevitable Trade-Offs

In every audit application, there are trade-offs between audit evidence, audit techniques, and use of audit personnel. These trade-offs are considered in the audit planning stage. During the implementation of the audit program, some trade-offs will be reconsidered. Flexibility in the audit program for closer inspection of some operational aspects may also require trade-off decisions. The audit management will document and control contingency plans when audit needs dictate them. Furthermore, because scope remains fixed once the engagement begins, evidence and techniques to fulfill audit objectives necessarily will be tailored to fit the scope. All of these factors mean that the audit program personnel must meet and exchange ideas regularly and be prepared to alter the program to obtain the best audit evidence and analysis possible within the given resources. The time/cost/event chart will reflect any changes made in the audit program.

The audit program may be conceptualized by looking at the bidirectional relationships in the investigation. These are depicted in Figure 3.4.

Back-and-Forth Relationships

Methodology: The bidirectional relationships must be taken into account in the methodology of the performance audit. First, policy objectives must be translated, by the performance auditor in conjunction with management, into measurable outputs. These outputs may be straightforward in some instances, e.g., beds filled in a hospital, or student enrollments in a public university. However, in most instances, they require qualitative, expert judgment assessments, e.g., *necessary* operations for hospital patients, and a *relevant* education for university students. The performance auditor, in these nonquantitative assessments, must define "necessary" and "relevant" in operational terms. Then the evaluation by the performance auditor can take place. Furthermore, the definition of outputs in operational terms has a beneficial effect on management and fosters self-assessment by management. The utility of having performance auditors and managers jointly involved in defining outputs rests largely on objectivity and the multi-disciplinary approach taken by the audit team. By committing themselves to the output goals management is more effective in controlling and directing the resources and personnel in the organizational unit.

Figure 3.4
Bi-Directional Relationships in a Performance Audit Investigation

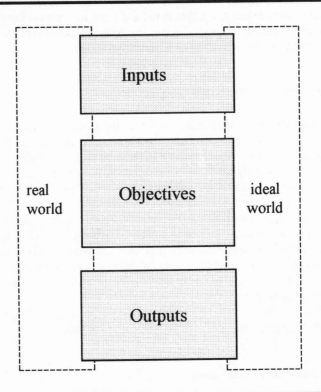

Objectives: In conjunction with the specification of outputs, however, objectives themselves must be operationalized. Varying interpretations of objectives will lead to different specifications of outputs. Therefore, a concomitant chore of the performance audit team is to examine the statements of policy objectives for clarity, quality, and quantity dimensions. Examination of the policy objectives may lead to better specification of policy, more clear statements of objectives, more coherence between policies, and closer adherence of policy statements for the organizational unit to the total business environment. In this examination no attempt is made by the performance auditor to change policy; rather, the emphasis is on the integrity of the policy statements and communication of policy. The relationship is bidirectional, then, in the following way: availability of inputs tempers the definition of objectives (forward-looking), while the general policy statements about objectives lead to a description of inputs needed (backward-looking). Policy statements do not typically imply the availability of goods and services to meet the policy; fulfilling policy occurs in the real world in accordance with the laws of supply and demand. Resources are supplied to the business unit and the owners/stakeholders in that unit demand value for that money. The performance audit communicates to the stakeholders the effectiveness of management in using resources.

Outputs: A second bidirectional relationship occurs between objectives and outputs. Policy objectives lead to the descriptions of measurable outputs of the business unit involved in the performance audit. These outputs must then be measured against actual performance; the extent of the variance between outputs demanded by the definition of policy objectives and the outputs supplied by the audit target lead the performance auditor to be able to express an opinion on the economy, efficiency, and effectiveness dimensions. The bidirectionality in the performance audit in the second phase of the audit program, then, involves defining outputs from objectives and then comparing actual outputs with the specified objectives. The objectives to outputs stage is forward-looking, while the output back to objectives stage is backward-looking.

Universal Methodology

In every performance audit the audit program will have similar characteristics regardless of the application. These characteristics are:

1. Consult with senior management or the audit committee;

2. perform a background analysis for familiarity with the audit target;

3. analyze internal controls as they apply to the audit application;

4. investigate for evidence of economy, efficiency, and effectiveness;

5. analyze the evidence in order to form recommendations, and an opinion, if an opinion is within the scope of the audit;

6. document the findings, prepare a report, communicate the findings and be prepared to testify as to the results of the audit.

AUDIT EVIDENCE

The prevailing philosophy for optimal information is: *comprehensive accounting fosters comprehensive auditing.* In order for the comprehensive audit to take place expeditiously, and in order for audit evidence to be found to support the performance audit, the depth and breadth of accounting data must change. One major change required is, of course, the backing away from reliance on historical data and the backing away from reliance on quantitative data. Instead, more pro-forma data is needed, as well as an emphasis on qualitative data.

Quantity and Relevance of Evidence

There are two distinct dimensions to consider with regard to the audit evidence for the performance audit. First, the evidence must be qualified; that is, the auditor must ask, "Is it relevant?" If it is relevant the evidence can become part of the paper trail toward the performance audit. Once evidence is qualified, a second dimension enters into the scene. That dimension asks, "If the evidence is relevant, how *much* of it is needed to form an expert opinion?" Qualification of evidence will typically be based on the audit program; the quantity dimension will usually be based on the degree to which internal controls can be relied upon.

The authority for the performance audit team to obtain evidence is based on the engagement letter; this letter, or authorization from an inspector general's office in many cases in the public sector, will specify the scope. Within the specified scope the performance audit team is authorized to obtain sufficient evidentiary matter. This may seem more self-evident in the abstract than in reality. In reality, there may be substantial resistance to the access to information by the performance audit team.

An Example

One recent case of interest concerns "product dumping" by Japan. "Dumping" occurs when a firm intentionally takes a loss on goods and services by selling them below cost. The purpose of this dumping is to drive a competitor out of the market, particularly if the dumping firm is large and financially sound and the competitor is a new and minimally capitalized entry into the market. For many years, many computer firms in the United States have accused the computer giant Fujitsu, of Japan, of dumping in the United States. However, access to the evidence which would substantiate or deny these suspicions has not been available. Now, after submitting a "competitive" bid to provide a computer system to the municipality of Hiroshima in Japan, Fujitsu is being accused of dumping inside its own territory. The bid was approximately one cent. The government has committed itself to obtain evidence and Fujitsu has withdrawn the offending bid. Evidence to substantiate dumping would include highly proprietary information, such as cost, overhead allocation, research and development expenditures, and the dealer mark-up. The ethics of reporting such information depends upon the accountability relationships. In this case, the firm will not want to risk the public exposure of such sensitive information to competitors. As this illustrates, in performance auditing, because of the variability of practice in the field, obtaining audit evidence may be more difficult than immediately apparent.

Types of Evidence

With regard to audit evidence, it is common to access information by

- interviews

- documents

- knowledgeable third parties

- comparative analyses

- manpower reviews (both by interviewing, as well as obtaining personnel performance reports)

- minutes of meetings

An overall system of audit evidence is shown in Figure 3.5.

Controls determine the extent of audit evidence needed; then a methodology can be developed. From that arises a stage of observing resource use. This resource use then becomes the raw data for looking at outputs. The outputs are subsequently compared to the objectives.

AUDIT ASSESSMENT, EVALUATION, AND METHODOLOGY

Given the somewhat *ad hoc* nature of performance auditing, specific methodologies are not forthcoming. However, some general guidelines can be provided. Since the evidence in the performance audit is both qualitative as well as quantitative, expert opinion, supported by audit evidence, is the most effective methodology available. The benefit/cost relationship will guide the auditor in determining how detailed or elaborate the evaluation should be. Furthermore, elegant statistical and analytical techniques are hardly justified if the audit evidence is "soft" or highly probabilistic to begin with.

The audit evaluation should include consideration of

- verification of evidence

- crossreference of evidence

- the interrelationships of the findings

The performance auditor should exercise extreme caution in inferring causality of effects. These issues may impute power to managers that they do not have.[6] Therefore, the performance auditor may want to maintain sensitivity to the

Figure 3.5
System of Audit Evidence

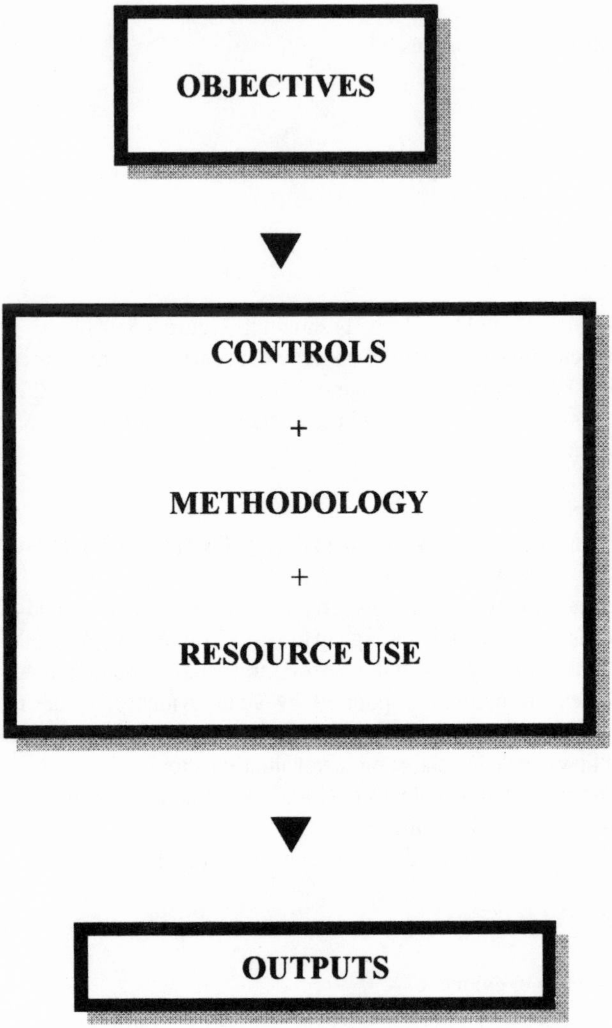

```
┌─────────────────────────────┐
│                             │
│        OBJECTIVES           │
│                             │
└─────────────────────────────┘

              ▼

┌───────────────────────────────────┐
│                                   │
│            CONTROLS               │
│                                   │
│               +                   │
│                                   │
│          METHODOLOGY              │
│                                   │
│               +                   │
│                                   │
│          RESOURCE USE             │
│                                   │
└───────────────────────────────────┘

              ▼

┌───────────────────────────────────┐
│            OUTPUTS                │
└───────────────────────────────────┘
```

environment in which management operates, and the degree of control which management can potentially exercise over resources.

An Evaluation Framework: Multinational Background

In assessing the evidence, the performance auditor will necessarily spend a great deal of effort on consideration of alternatives for improvements. This is, after all, the contribution of the performance audit product. Therefore, in the examination of evidence, the auditor will focus on other ways in which the management could have achieved the same objective (this emphasizes economy), or ways in which management could maximize outputs, given the resources they employed (this emphasizes efficiency), or ways in which the outputs could be enhanced or better fulfill objectives (this relates to effectiveness). By operating within this framework of evaluation the performance auditor provides explicit consideration of alternatives.

Canada and New Zealand have developed a specific methodology for the component parts of the performance audit function within the public sector. These component parts address the pervasive way in which governments serve constituents and provide a framework for the performance audit team. In Canada the acronym FRAME is used to define the model.[7] Canada's Office of the Auditor General, in the *Comprehensive Auditing Manual* and various specific *Audit Guides*, includes an attest function in the performance audit. While the acronym FRAME has not persisted in the Office of the Auditor General's publications[8] it is a useful indication of the general approach taken. The approach is to employ a methodology which includes Financial Controls, Reporting to Parliament, Attest and Authority, Management Controls, and EDP Controls. The Attest and Authority element specifies that an opinion will be rendered on the performance audit, and that the resources used were authorized by the Parliament or some other legitimate authority.

In New Zealand, the acronym developed for the elements of the performance audit in the public sector is CARE. The components are Control, Attest and Authority, Reporting, and Effectiveness and Efficiency. The New Zealand approach specifically fosters a complete and comprehensive audit of financial statements supplemented by a performance audit of certain, limited, aspects of a public office.[9] In both Canada and New Zealand these methodologies apply only to public sector audits at this time.

REPORTING AND THE ACCOUNTABILITY FUNCTIONS

While accountability has been discussed previously, it is a crucial element in the implementation scheme when discussing the reporting of the performance audit. This is because the reports must be addressed to the appropriate audience; in some cases, confidentiality must be maintained, while in others, the report should be comprehensible to anyone who might care to pick it up. Furthermore, the accountability is significant because the report should address the concerns articulated by the "contracting" party. For these reasons the accountability relationships should be explored prior to the undertaking of the performance audit; this is why the topic was handled earlier in this book. Some fundamental considerations in reporting are highlighted below.

To Whom?

The first issue to be addressed by the practitioner performance audit team in the reporting process will be to determine to whom the audit report should be addressed. In some public sector applications the report is issued to the legislature. In others, it goes to the inspector or auditor general of the agency containing the audit target. Some private sector reports will be addressed to boards of directors or other executives. In still other cases, the performance audit may be commissioned by an external party, such as a bank or other lending or capital financing agency. For example, the World Bank and the United Nations often request comprehensive auditing for the accountability of the funding they provide. The engagement letter should provide definitive information on the intended recipients of the report.

What To Report?

The second issue to be addressed is the amount and type of information to be contained in the report. Where the report is confidential, the quality and quantity of information contained in the report will be different than the reports issued for public accountability to legislatures. And while not impugning the dignity and sophistication of legislatures, the auditor may wish to keep technical jargon to an absolute minimum if the target of the report represents a broad range of talents. After all, the report only holds the agency accountable if the recommendations are clearly outlined and readily comprehended.

When?

Finally, the report must be submitted in a timely manner. There will be no impact if the report reaches the elected officials after the enactment of a subsequent budget. Similarly, if the board of directors has already renewed the contracts of key operating officers, the performance audit report will be one more two-inch wide document on a dusty bookshelf. The audit report should reach decision makers in time to influence their actions, and allow them to operate in a *proactive* environment.

Good News, Bad News

Another general issue to consider in preparing performance audit reports is the public relations effect of the document. One critical beneficial aspect of the report is that it assures the providers of capital, whether they are taxpayers or shareholders, that the organization is proceeding about their business in a largely appropriate manner. That is, the report provides assurance that the organization is "healthy" and that resources are being utilized reasonably. This is a positive public relations function, and experts in the performance audit area stress that, rather than a focus on the negative, a well-written and well-organized performance audit report will disseminate findings on the positive aspects of operational successes. These successes may be the existence and operational effectiveness of internal controls, the maintenance of the "economy" dimension in contracting for goods and services, the general fulfillment of organizational goals, the overall contribution of the audit target to the entire operation, or whatever.

The well-known article on "moral mazes" in management[10] labels the syndrome of management attempts to avoid blame as indicative of poor corporate tracking of management, and the absence of well-defined lines of responsibility:[11]

There is no more feared hour in the corporate world than "blame time." Blame is quite different from responsibility. There is a cartoon of Richard Nixon declaring: 'I accept all of the responsibility, but none of the blame.' To blame someone is to injure him verbally in public; in large organizations, where one's image is crucial, this poses the most serious sort of threat. For managers, blame—like failure—has nothing to do with the merits of a case; it is a matter of social definition. As a general rule, it is those who are or who become politically vulnerable or expendable who get 'set up' and become blamable. The most feared situation of all is to end up inadvertently in the wrong place at the wrong time and get blamed.

With regard to the performance audit report, the recommendations and the criticisms alike should apply to management as a whole, rather than attacking specific or identifiable managers. If any other approach is taken, the "blame time" syndrome is likely to prevail. Seen as a part of the entire performance audit process, the report is a notification to the accountable parties that certain systems are in control, and others are out-of-control. Bringing the out of control systems back into control is the responsibility of management *as a whole*, and will be monitored by various personnel within the organization.

AUDIT REPORT CONTENT

The audit report should include details on accountability relationships, the scope of the audit, the methodology employed in approaching the performance audit, the qualifications of the key audit management personnel, and the audit objectives. These preliminary details set the expectations for the performance audit for the reader of the report.

Subsequent to the background information, the audit results themselves are presented. The Canadian Comprehensive Auditing Foundation suggests that the report be preceded with a section which presents an overview of the "themes" of the audit.[12] Themes are repetitive findings which have been found to exist throughout the audit target. Or they may be repetitive support elements which provide evidence for the recommendations made in the report. Within these themes are findings which must be documented and recommendations for improvements. As mentioned above, positive as well as negative findings should be included in the report.

Recommendations of the Auditors

Recommendations, when made, should be concrete and articulated in a way that they can be easily operationalized. That is, the recommendations should indicate:

- how to correct deficiencies

- who should perform the correction

- who should monitor the correction

- how to measure the correction progress

- at what point the correction has succeeded, and how to measure when the system is back "in control."

Management's Responsibility to Respond

Management should have the opportunity to issue a report in conjunction with the performance audit report. There are several reasons why this appeal is made to practicing performance auditors. First, another public relations function is served: the public knows that management is aware of, and willing to correct, deficiencies in economy, efficiency, and effectiveness. Second, management has a different perspective than the auditor and may want to appeal for additional resources or reallocation of resources in conjunction with the recommendations provided in the audit report. Third, allowing management to alternately compliment themselves or make legitimate excuses for shortcomings falls within the category of gentlemanly behavior; the performance auditor does not need to be an adversary of management to be effective as an auditor.

Acknowledgment of Limitations

Audit limitations should be addressed; these may be limitations in either scope or in audit evidence. This limitations statement can be made either in the preface material to the audit report or after the recommendations are presented. Clearly, limitations which affect the scope in a material way will simultaneously affect the issuance of any audit opinion contained in the report. Limitations of this significance would clearly be more appropriately presented at the beginning of the performance audit report than the end.

In some nations performance auditing is well-developed. Formal, promulgated standards exist and an attest function is sometimes permitted. Under these circumstances, the audit report should state that the audit was performed in conformity with performance audit standards, and the opinion should be presented within the recommendations and format of the standards.[13]

Special Considerations

Two observations may be made at this point. First, because of the significant amount of resources in the human asset category today, in both the labor-intensive public sector, as well as the rapidly-growing service industries in the private sector, special consideration should be devoted to human assets in the performance audit. Knowledge workers are particularly difficult to model and therefore their outputs or "effectiveness" criteria are extremely resistant to measurement. However, because of the materiality of the dollars spent in acquiring, training, and retaining the services of knowledge workers, the performance audit should take special effort to address manpower management.

The second observation concerns the role of the internal auditor in the performance audit arena, but especially with regard to the audit reporting function. The advent of the widespread application of performance auditing points toward a much stronger role for the internal auditor than in the past. By definition, the internal auditor concerns him or herself with the system of controls within an organization. As such, the implementation of the recommendations presented in the performance audit report will come under the purview of the internal auditor. It will become a part of the internal auditor's responsibility to monitor, measure, and report on the extent to which the recommendations in the performance audit have been implemented. In a sense, the internal auditor will now have to insert a second layer of controls, i.e., those which correspond to the realization of the goals set out in the performance audit report. These goals may be supplementary to those set out by management. As such, the controls for the supplementary portion may compose a separate system. The internal auditor is therefore well-advised to prepare for the future by internalizing the system of performance auditing. A strong contribution by the internal audit staff can be made in conjunction with the performance audit report and this significant influence should be recognized in the education and practice cases of existing and future internal auditors. Internal audit staff resources will need to keep pace with these increasing responsibilities.

NOTES

1. D. R. Sheldon and E. F. McNamara. *Value-For-Money Auditing in the Public Sector*. Altamonte Springs, FL: Institute of Internal Auditors. 1991. p. 13.

2. This terminology is from *Public Sector Auditing Statement #4, Value-for-Money Auditing Standards*, March 1988, of the Public Sector Accounting and Auditing Committee

of the Canadian Institute of Chartered Accountants.

3. The AICPA has made the point in their *Industry Audit Guide on Audits of State and Local Governments* (Committee on Governmental Accounting and Auditing, Third Edition, American Institute of Certified Public Accountants, 1981) that the vastly improved quality of accounting in the public sector has largely resulted from the better control of the governments through the use of independent audits. They assert: "There have also been significant developments which encourage the extension of audit engagements to include reporting on compliance and performance areas," p. 5.

4. Sir Douglas Henley, Clive Holtham, Andrew Likierman, and John Perrin. *Public Sector Accounting and Financial Control*. The Chartered Institute of Public Finance and Accountancy, Berkshire, England: Van Nostrand Reinhold (UK). 1983.

5. Layfield Committee. *Local Government Finance: Report of the Committee of Enquiry*. CMNd. 6453, England: HMSO. 1976, p. 102.

6. James Cutt discusses technical/financial/economic analytic methods in *Comprehensive Auditing in Canada: Theory and Practice*. New York: Praeger. 1988. pp. 139 ff. Partial technical/financial/economic methodologies evaluate the organization unit being audited as a unit alone; in a partial t/f/e analysis the auditor can use either a single objective or a multiple objective method. In a general, rather than partial t/f/e analysis, the organization is viewed by the auditor as a dynamic and interactive part of a larger group providing multiple goods and services. The effect of using the various t/f/e analytic models translates, for all practical purposes to the auditor, into the breadth and depth of either or both quantitative and qualitative performance measures.

7. Some specialized references in this area include guidelines from the Auditor General's office and from the Canadian Comprehensive Auditing Foundation. In particular, see: Auditor General of Canada. Audit Guide. *Auditing of Procedures for Effectiveness*. Ottawa: Auditor General of Canada. (August 1981); also, *Auditing for Effectiveness*. Ottawa: Auditor General of Canada. (August 1981); and Audit Guide. *Auditing of Efficiency*. Ottawa: Auditor General of Canada (January 1981); in addition, Canadian Comprehensive Auditing Foundation. *Comprehensive Auditing: Concepts, Components, and Characteristics*. Ottawa, 1983; Canadian Comprehensive Auditing Foundation. *Value for Money in Municipalities: a Practitioner's Guide to Municipal Comprehensive Auditing*. Ottawa: CCAF. 1984. For Crown Corporations in Canada, Bill C-24 (September 1, 1984) as an amendment to the Financial Administration Act, contains useful information.

8. Cutt. 1988. p. 223.

9. John J. Glynn. *Value for Money Auditing in the Public Sector. Research Studies in Accounting*. Series edited by B. V. Carsberg. Englewood Cliffs, NJ: Prentice Hall. 1985. p. 129.

10. Robert Jackall, well-known for the term "moral mazes," has an easy-to-read book on the subject: *Moral Mazes: The World of Corporate Managers*. London: Oxford University Press. 1988.

11. Robert Jackall. "Moral Mazes: Bureaucracy and Managerial Work." In *Ethics in Practice: Managing the Moral Corporation*. Kenneth R. Andrews, ed. Boston: Harvard Business School Press. 1989. p. 117.

12. The Canadian Comprehensive Auditing Foundation has a broad range of publications, but a particularly succinct one which introduces the suggestion of "themes" is: *Comprehensive Auditing: Concepts, Components and Characteristics*. Ottawa: Canadian Comprehensive Auditing Foundation. 6th Printing. Undated. The Foundation's literature in this area is extensive and is significantly devoted to applications in government and quasi-government applications.

13. For example, performance auditing standards in Canada are issued by the Public Sector

Accounting and Auditing Committee of the Canadian Institute of Chartered Accountants. See: *Public Sector Auditing Statement #4, Value-for-Money Auditing Standards.* March 1988.

Chapter 4

Pulling Together in the Same Direction: Performance Auditing in a Total Quality Management Environment

INTRODUCTION

The popular press and professional literature are replete with admonitions to public and private entities to achieve total quality management. Organizations wish to caress the public into understanding that they are downsizing, streamlining, and enhancing productivity. They release information to the marketplace that they are fully engaged in a total quality management environment. Sometimes the technique is slightly different, or the term varies (we are seeing more "benchmarking" and "re-engineering" in the private sector as well as "management by objectives" or "reinventing government" in the public sector). But the message is the same: the entity is striving for accountability to its shareholders or constituents by some variant of a technique to apply explicit attention to achieving strategic goals. In this chapter the interface between total quality management (TQM) and performance auditing is explored. The two approaches are highly synergistic, and, in combination, produce accountability with more clarity than ever before.

TQM THEORY AND OBJECTIVES

Today, with increasingly vociferous shareholders and taxpayers, more competitiveness in both a domestic and global environment, reduced corporate profitability rates, and diminished urban tax bases, creating an organizational climate for enhanced productivity is paramount. In addition, with reduced trade barriers and the opening of previously "closed" international economies, products, markets, and profits shift rapidly like desert sands. Successful leadership demands the ability to respond quickly and with agility to changing consumer demands.

Total Quality Management (TQM) arose as a complement to statistical process control (SPC). SPC was found to be a rather successful technique enabling top and midlevel managers to focus on a finite number of qualitative objectives which were then quantitatively measured. This permitted the comparison of goals and reality in a qualitative way, much like comparison between budgets and actual expenditures provide feedback on financial objectives. In effect, the traditional focus on internal financial controls, reducing expenditures, and enhancing profitability, was simply too limiting in the growing and more dynamic world economy. SPC, relying on teams and nonfinancial management leadership, works basically like this:

1. Functional areas have responsibility for discovering critical processes;

2. processes are charted and quantified by each management team;

3. managers are trained in acquiring and charting data; mathematical techniques are taught;

4. interpreting and reporting of data is achieved by management teams;

5. as the processes are monitored, achievements, problems, and improvement plans are discussed by the teams;

6. documentation is a key element of success.

TQM was initially adopted in Japan, after exposure by Americans. The most popular names associated with TQM are W. Edwards Deming, Kaoru Ishikawa, Joseph Juran, Armand Feigenbaum, and Philip Crosby. In order to implement TQM, group dynamics are usually enhanced by brainstorming sessions or other techniques.

Reengineering

Some experts are predicting that TQM will soon be replaced as a popular technique for quality management by corporate reengineering. Reengineering is another philosophy which dictates restructuring of the entity into critical processes and adds the dimension of particular attention to redundancy of processes, materials, and people to the performance system. The team concept, the empowerment of employees at all levels, and the requirement of entity-wide commitment to the process are characteristics that reengineering shares with TQM. Where it parts company is in its attention to resource use: achieving the most with the least input while maintaining quality. Thus, reengineering enhances TQM by the measurement and reporting of inputs and outputs both quantitatively and qualitatively.

At a minimum level of complexity, TQM may be summarized by attention to five steps:

1. The entire organization must be trained and committed to the TQM philosophy for

the technique to prevail;

2. an assessment is made of the current placement of the organization in its present environment;

3. a blueprint is prepared by entity-wide participation of where the organization would like to be placed in the future; an appraisal of what the future environment will look like is performed;

4. the pathway to achieving the future position is delineated in steps and goals;

5. constant, explicit, and detailed analysis is performed on where the organization is, how far it has come toward its future vision, and whether the future vision needs to be adjusted.

The most frequently mentioned impediment to the use of TQM includes failure to get the entire organization committed to the philosophy and technique. This may be a particularly acute flaw in an entity characterized by a traditional bureaucracy. In this setting, traditionally-trained managers have great difficulty trusting and adjusting to the new TQM environment.

TQM requires extensive and expensive training for success. The achievements under TQM must be known and rewarded for total entity commitment to flourish. Key factors in successful implementation include knowing who the customers are and what they want. In certain environments, such as the public sector, this alone may present an insurmountable obstacle to embarking on a TQM conversion. Even more difficult is the need to provide employees with the tools, resources, and ability to make the changes that TQM demands. With profit margins being squeezed, allocating additional resources may be unrealistic, and empowering employees to take risks with resources may be inadvisable.

Client Focus

The client focus of TQM aims to continually improve products and services so that market share can climb. Documentation of improvements in quality is a key component of the system. In delineating key programs and processes for the achievement of better customer satisfaction, entity-wide teams need to distinguish between two kinds of organizational problems: systemic or episodic. Many goods and services quality measurements can be measured and reports generated.

In the application of TQM, a major distinction is the focus on the customer. The issue of customer satisfaction becomes the driver deciding critical processes and plans. In traditional economic theory, management operates to maximize shareholder wealth. Managers are surrogates for shareholders in operating the entity to enhance financial rewards to owners, while minimizing the riskiness to the investor. In this theoretical environment, managers direct and control the organization to achieve financial goals.

Even companies whose experience with TQM has been highly positive are still largely at a loss to correlate changes in market dominance or value-of-the-firm criteria with the TQM process. Furthermore, the relationship between corporate revenue and TQM remains shrouded in a haze of many complex variables which are difficult to break down or to assign a causality factor. Do satisfied customers buy more, or do they just have more brand loyalty? If patented technology intervenes will a satisfied customer dump loyalty for an improved product? Is a satisfied customer willing to pay a higher price for the satisfaction, enhancing producer profitability?

On the other hand, TQM is fundamentally at odds with the economic model of management working for shareholders in a stewardship function. Shareholder wealth and customer satisfaction may not bear a direct relationship. In the application of TQM, management must surrender authority to employees at every level throughout the organization.

Management's job is to collect and disseminate the goals and achievements of teams of workers. This implies a complete redesigning of work assignments and performance reviews. The role of management changes requiring an entity-wide commitment to the new philosophy.

Shareholder wealth takes a back seat in favor of focus on the customer. The strategic goals are set by the entire population of the entity and are those related to consumer satisfaction. Successful implementation of TQM in companies such as Xerox, Hewlett-Packard, Allen-Bradley, and Banc One has been achieved because of systemic agreement in the corporate culture to commit to TQM.[1]

Modification of Traditional Economic Theory under TQM

TQM is a difficult commitment to make if you are a traditional manager who likes to direct and control as taught in business schools a decade back. In particular, where financial controls are tight, and profitability is on a tight margin, managers may experience particular angst relinquishing control. It is risky to empower employees to make decisions independent of top management which may affect the firm's reported financial position. The technique of benchmarking to assess goals and performance replaces traditional financial budgeting and controls. In effect, the stewardship function of management under traditional economic theory, wherein managers act in the interests of shareholders, is extinct. Now, instead, TQM substitutes customer satisfaction as a surrogate for traditional financial performance; under TQM, teams of employees rather than top-down managers are charged with achieving customer goals. In fact, the only top-down management trend in a TQM environment is the insistence of management that the TQM philosophy must reign throughout the organization, and that adherence to TQM will be rewarded at all levels of employment. For the organizational climate to thrive, there must be a minimum of time between the training of workers in the TQM program and the opportunity to apply it.

In replacing the traditional economic theory of the firm with TQM, the capital marketplace must adopt a longer-range horizon for matching management policy and market returns to shareholders. In fact, the very relationship between customer satisfaction and market returns is tenuous and largely not researched at present. Baldrige award-winning companies, for example, have been able to thrive in the marketplace by a focus on consumer satisfaction and gaining consumer market share by adjusting to market changes and market demands effectively. But "continuous improvement" goals of the TQM process do not appear to have been realized among U.S. companies; rather, the majority show improvements over a few years followed by a plateau, while a very small proportion demonstrate the "continuous improvement" sought by the TQM philosophy.[2] In fact, companies such as Westinghouse Electric, IBM, Texas Instruments Defense Systems, and Federal Express Corporation, are examples of highly successful implementation of TQM; however, the rate of gains appears to have flattened out relatively quickly. There are two ways (or, at least two ways) to interpret this information. First, it may be that as all companies adopt TQM and become more competitive, the competitive advantage of TQM is lost; the TQM standard becomes the basic standard of performance. Second, it may be that TQM offers a quick and demonstrable ratcheting up of performance, but is a one-time gain (although, the time horizon for the one-time may be a period of several years). In either case, TQM may not offer shareholders subscribing to the traditional economic model of the firm much solace.

PERFORMANCE AUDIT THEORY AND OBJECTIVES

Since chapter 3 develops the implementation of performance audit, and chapter 2 discusses its objectives, a review of the theoretical constructs of performance auditing will suffice here. The purpose of this discourse is to provide a basis for the amalgamation of TQM and performance auditing. Let's begin with a summary of a general audit conceptual model, the most popular of several competing theories.

The principal-agent model views relationships between managers and owners in the private sector, or managers and taxpayers in the public sector. The principals are those with residual ownership rights (stockholders in the private sector, taxpayers in the public sectors) and the agents are the managers who are employed to act in absentia for the principals. There are four basic compromises in the principal-agent relationship:

1. conflict of interest

2. consequence

3. complexity

4. remoteness[3]

Conflict of interest arises from the fact that the managers may act in their own self-interest rather than that of the principals. This interjects an unnecessary "cost" in the principal-agent relationship that would not exist if the principals acted on their own behalf. For example, in recent years we have seen the rise of managements taking public firms private, often by shafting the shareholders. In some cases managements have disgruntled shareholders in favor of bondholders. In still other scenarios managements whose compensation is based on increases in earnings per share will sacrifice the overall valuation of the firm in favor of short-term corporate earnings, which in turn enhance the salaries of managers.

These conflicts lead principals to seek assurance that managers are acting in the interest of the owners/stakeholders, and that the information provided by the agents to the principals is relatively free from bias. The audit, performed by an independent third party, provides such assurance at a reasonable cost to the principals. Furthermore, knowing that there will be an audit which will be reported to the principals, agents are dissuaded from dysfunctional behavior.

The compromise of *consequence* in the principal-agent paradigm refers to the inequality of information between principals and agents. Agents as insiders have extensive knowledge which is not imparted in financial statements and other public information. Rather, the primary source of information for principals is the annual report of the firm, supplemented by other public disclosures. This means that the agents' annual report and accompanying disclosures have considerable "consequence" to the principals, and others who have a relationship with the firm, such as creditors, suppliers, and regulators. To protect this information from misstatement or bias, principals gladly pay the audit fees to receive assurance that the information is free from material misstatement, and is prepared in accordance with professional standards which make comparability to other similar entities possible.

Complexity has several dimensions which relate to the principal-agent relationship. First, complexity of reported information makes it difficult for principals to interpret. Second, the inherent complexity of the entity makes it difficult for the agents to summarize effectively in a finite and professionally proscribed report format. Third, the very act of collapsing a high volume of complicated data into a preordained reporting requirement entails errors of omission, uncertainties, and filtered-out but relevant detail. The cost of the audit to the principals is justified by the extent to which auditors judge the quality of the information provided. As such, principals benefit from knowing that material information is not omitted and that the information as presented is free of material errors.

The last element of compromise in the principal-agent relationship is that of *remoteness*. Since the principal must rely on the agent to produce data and is not able to directly observe the data source, he absorbs both the costs of simplification and the inability to verify data. In utilizing an auditor, the principal recaptures the decisions made by the agent in simplification as well as the ability to examine the source data. The auditor performs these functions at a cost to the principal to enable the stakeholders to have confidence in the integrity of the reported elements of financial statements.

In the principal-agent theory financial statements themselves serve the purpose of providing information to present and potential participants in the capital marketplace. As these participants evaluate the reported information they are able to determine how to allocate their capital by making selections along a risk/reward continuum. The risk/reward continuum outlines the myriad choices of investments, given the observation that increased rewards or returns are achievable only by increasing the level of risk. That is, there is a risk premium or cost associated with above average returns. However within each risk class the participant will want to achieve the highest reward available for any specified risk class. A simplified version or surrogate of risk is often assumed to be variability of returns. Therefore, the principals' reliance on comparable and consistently prepared public reports is significant. Principals look to auditors to provide assurance that the reports are reasonably reliable.

The key element of the audit report is that it provides credibility to the representations of management. Management is responsible for making decisions on operations, maintaining an information system as well as a system of internal control, and reporting to external parties. Auditors, in turn, use procedures which are relatively standardized in concept, but rely upon professional judgment to apply in order to extend believability to the representations of management. The cost of the audit is justified by the enhanced credibility of the reports. In a performance audit, management is held accountable for conducting operations economically, efficiently, and effectively. The audit, performed by an independent third party from the principals and agents, helps the capital market to operate with better reliability.

INTERFACING TQM WITH PERFORMANCE AUDITING

TQM does not work effectively if new performance requirements are instituted on top of existing ones. The emphasis on quality and consumer satisfaction must thoroughly saturate the company and replace traditional economic goals. The TQM system breaks down where performance auditing picks up. That is, TQM looks at results by benchmarking resources applied to achieve a goal. Performance auditing looks at *effective* use of resources, and whether the result could have been achieved with fewer resources, less expensive resources, or a better mix of resources. The quality objective of TQM is modified, when the performance audit philosophy is added, to be lowest-cost quality with the most efficient use of scarce resources. Acquisition of technology, often dictated by the TQM process, is only rewarded under performance auditing when it demonstrably enhances least-cost quality.

Data Issues in TQM

Consider, for example, the case study of the Martin Marietta Energy Group, which implemented TQM. A decision was made to base the assessment of the TQM philosophy in Martin Marietta Energy on the seven performance measures suggested by the Malcolm Baldrige National Quality Award.[4] The measures used were:

1. Employee ratings of supervisors' implementation of TQM;

2. proportion of employees trained in TQM;

3. time and money reductions;

4. quantity of interviews for benchmarking standards of nonfirm and competitive companies;

5. proportion of employees working in TQM teams;

6. existence of consumer satisfaction program with measurement and reporting;

7. quantity of ventures for improvement undertaken and executed.

These standards, taken as a whole, provide useful and relevant data in examining the success of the TQM program. In each dimension, the reporting standard scales the pervasiveness of TQM in the corporate environment. However, in each case, the emphasis is on what the organization achieved, without much reflection on what it was possible to achieve. Consider, for example, that even if 96 percent of employees are trained for TQM, we don't know if they were well-trained, or if they will use TQM, or if the training was accomplished at excessive cost. In addition, in standard seven, more ventures for improvement are not necessarily better. Were all of the ventures necessary, and were they successful? Was there an alternative which was more efficient to accomplish the same result than the actual ventures undertaken? Were these ventures worth the money when looking at costs and benefits? And, with standard four, was the quality of information obtained for benchmarking relevant, reliable, and obtained at least cost? Were the contacts worth the effort? Was anything accomplished with the data obtained for benchmarking? Was the data actually effectively used in the measurement and reporting system? In short, TQM measures quality and customer satisfaction gains, and performance audit adds accountability for use of resources.

In the TQM prototype, Deming dismisses quantification of goals as ineffective for either revealing performance or for motivating people. This assertion, however, is not supported by years of management research which have linked quantifiable goals to corporate achievements. In a rather comprehensive review of the research on this issue, at a time when over 500 studies have investigated the standard of goal setting, measurement, and review paradigm, the inscrutability of TQM cannot be sustained. Goal-setting theory as expounded by Edwin Locke in the 1960s appears to be at least as successful.[5] In addition, traditional management by objectives (MBO) as practiced in both the private and public sector over twenty years ago, may be more sustainable over the long run than TQM. Qualitative goals alone may not provide the educational or training benefit to employees that qualitative and quantitative controls together produce.[6]

The Baldrige Awards

While both TQM and performance auditing have been around for decades, an escalation in the popularity and implementation of both was seen in the late 1980s. President Ronald Reagan, capitalizing on the escalating interest in U.S. competitveness, disclosed the first Baldrige Award winners in November 1988. The Baldrige Awards were signed into law as Public Law 100-107 in 1987 as the U.S. National Quality Awards administered by The National Institute of Standards and Technology and the Secretary of Commerce. Armand Feigenbaum, widely recognized as a TQM expert, articulates six factors in accomplishing quality:[7]

- continuous quality requires new and innovative techniques

- quality is a discipline and a methodology like finance, accounting, and marketing

- quality is defined by the buyer, not by the seller

- quality is achieved by being adopted as a work ethic

- quality consists of processes integrated everywhere in the organization

- quality requires extensive teamwork

In short, TQM is a philosophy of management, producing an operational strategy which takes as a focus client satisfaction and quality of goods and services. It is forward-looking, since opportunities for new markets and new products must be explored to increase the market share of the firm.

In contrast, performance auditing is a set of processes which measure, evaluate, and report on economy, efficiency, and effectiveness of the firm's goals and achievements. It looks at performance already achieved, but provides input into changes needed for the future. Internal and external dimensions overlap as seen in Figure 4.1.

Benchmarking

The TQM strategy of benchmarking, which, on a continuous basis, compares the firm to its competitors, provides a basis for measurement. In many ways this is used in performance auditing, in which auditors obtain background information about the entity being audited, similar entities, and the environment in which it operates, in order to form expectations. Benchmarking both provides standards and demonstrates elements that have fostered success in others. For example, benchmarking involves collecting information from literature, experts internal and external to the firm, trade standards, competitors, professional organizations, and consultants. Performance auditors use similar information to gain knowledge about the auditee in comparison

Figure 4.1
Commonalities Between TQM and Performance Auditing: Inside the Entity

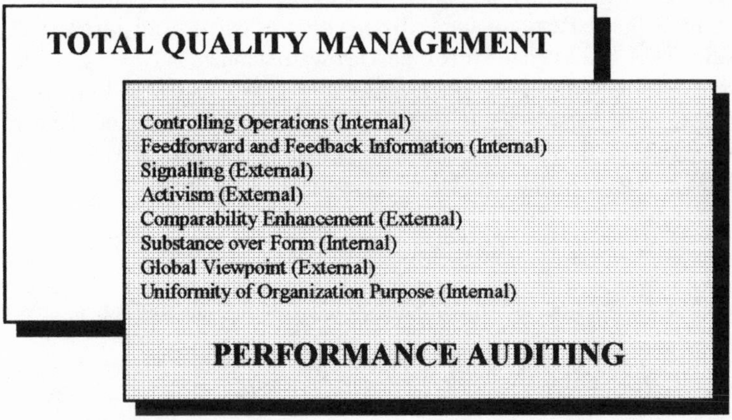

TOTAL QUALITY MANAGEMENT

Controlling Operations (Internal)
Feedforward and Feedback Information (Internal)
Signalling (External)
Activism (External)
Comparability Enhancement (External)
Substance over Form (Internal)
Global Viewpoint (External)
Uniformity of Organization Purpose (Internal)

PERFORMANCE AUDITING

with similar entities to look for variances and unexplained differences.

Benchmarking is a key component of TQM. First, the organization, by working in teams, sets out to diagnose the critical components of quality in the environment in which they operate. This would generally entail observing the entity itself, its competitors, and the global marketplace in which it operates. The observations, in turn, lead to the development of standards of performance; the entity is now in a position to compare and contrast its key components with others. This resulting information is disseminated throughout the organization to teams who are committed to implementing TQM in the organization (Figure 4.2).

While there are many permutations and combinations of data elements which may be relevant in benchmarking, a generic strategic would be to benchmark processes and product or service standards. Processes would include personnel related background, action, and review: training, team facilitating, communicating, empowerment and action-orientation, rewarding, and instilling a work ethic. To benchmark standards a review of markets, products, services, distribution, and research and development would provide a strong starting position. As the benchmarks are obtained and disseminated, the entity comes into the position of readiness to implement TQM (Figure 4.3) and scope issues are addressed (Figure 4.4).

Where TQM and Performance Audit Diverge

After comparing the similarities between benchmarking for TQM and the background analysis for performance audit, a comparison begins to diverge. Figure

Figure 4.2
Benchmarking Technique

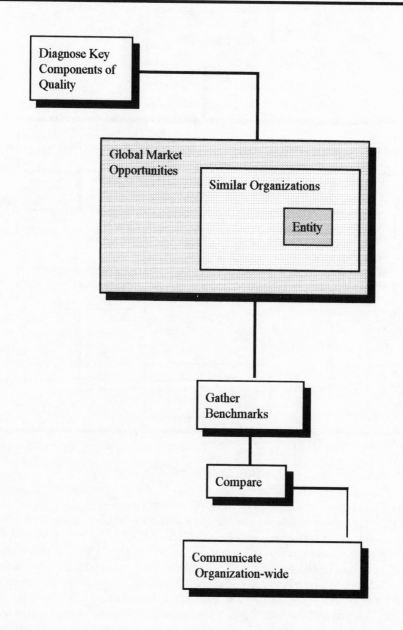

Diagnose Key Components of Quality

Global Market Opportunities

Similar Organizations

Entity

Gather Benchmarks

Compare

Communicate Organization-wide

Figure 4.3
Elements to Be Benchmarked

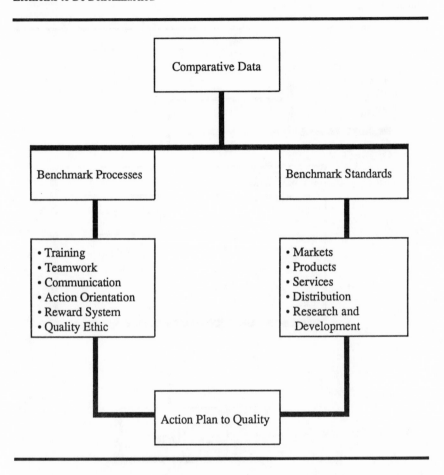

4.5 depicts the differences between TQM and performance audit.

While both TQM and performance audit may be characterized by the Ford Motor Company strategy (plan, do, check, act),[8] the elements are distinct. The objective of TQM is to run the organization in such a way that client satisfaction is maintained and enhanced, while performance auditing's objective is to evaluate the elements of performance. The mode of the techniques is, then, divergent; TQM is an operational system, while performance audit is a feedback and feedforward system of evaluation. And while TQM must be implemented entity-wide in teams of empowered employees, performance audit uses independent (primarily external) specialists to perform its work. The depth of the technique is extended to entity-wide processes in TQM, while performance audit targets specific areas of performance risk where the audit benefits will exceed its costs. Furthermore, as generally seen in TQM, the process addressed

Figure 4.4
Scope Considerations in Performance Audit

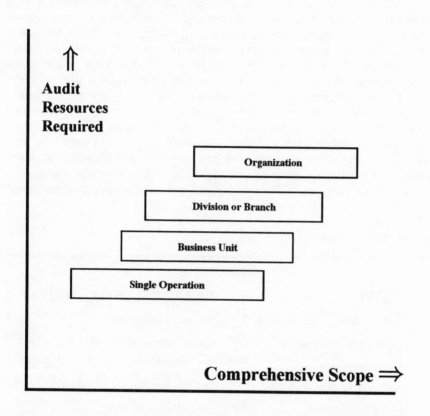

is a client satisfaction and quality plan, while the performance audit process is an audit plan (see chapter 3). Finally, TQM reports internally, while performance audits reports are prepared primarily for external audiences.

To interface the two techniques, a look at commonalities and differences demonstrates that while both are techniques to enhance performance, to provide feedback, and to improve management, performance audit takes as its focus accountability to stakeholders, while TQM adopts as its focus internal performance maintenance and development with a specific view toward customers.

Figure 4.6 articulates the significant distinctions and commonalities between performance auditing and total quality management by functions.

Deficiencies of Traditional Accounting Reports

We know that TQM has caught on, in part, because the traditional management accounting reports have not achieved the level of performance that today's organizations have desired. This is true even though management accounting has had several significant advances relatively recently. Some of these are activity-based costing, life-cycle costing, and through-put accounting. Activity-based costing, developed from the concepts put forth by Robert Kaplan and Robin Cooper at Harvard Business School in the late 1980s, adopts the TQM concept of continuous improvement. Product costing and profitability performance is assessed under activity-based costing by attention to indirect costs and the cost drivers that influence them. The method permits more relevant costs to be developed by unbundling overhead and allocating to products or processes. The technique is even more of a significant innovation when it is noted that, while most indirect costs have been allocated on the basis of labor, labor today may comprise a very insignificant part of total cost. For example, labor constitutes an average of eight percent of product costs for companies using just-in-time methods, and is just four percent at Tektronix, and

Figure 4.5
Differences in TQM and Performance Audit

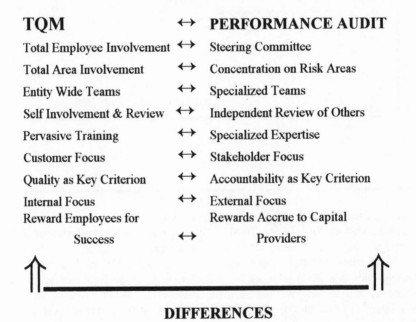

TQM	↔	PERFORMANCE AUDIT
Total Employee Involvement	↔	Steering Committee
Total Area Involvement	↔	Concentration on Risk Areas
Entity Wide Teams	↔	Specialized Teams
Self Involvement & Review	↔	Independent Review of Others
Pervasive Training	↔	Specialized Expertise
Customer Focus	↔	Stakeholder Focus
Quality as Key Criterion	↔	Accountability as Key Criterion
Internal Focus	↔	External Focus
Reward Employees for Success	↔	Rewards Accrue to Capital Providers

DIFFERENCES

Figure 4.6
Comprehensive Framework of TQM and Performance Audit

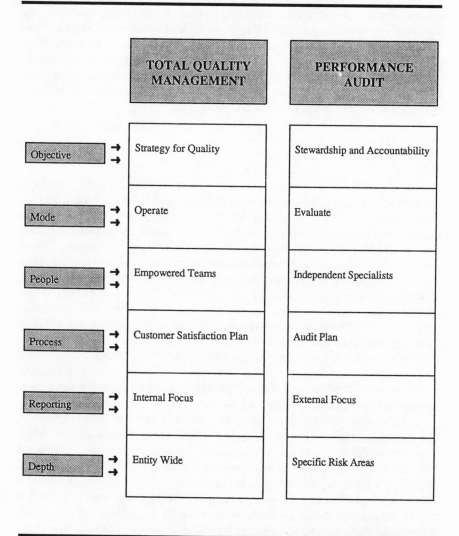

	TOTAL QUALITY MANAGEMENT	PERFORMANCE AUDIT
Objective	Strategy for Quality	Stewardship and Accountability
Mode	Operate	Evaluate
People	Empowered Teams	Independent Specialists
Process	Customer Satisfaction Plan	Audit Plan
Reporting	Internal Focus	External Focus
Depth	Entity Wide	Specific Risk Areas

two percent at Hewlett-Packard.[9] Life-cycle costing arose because the actual manufacturing phase of production today is no longer the significant time period; rather, the more relevant period includes the typically longer research and design time, which also absorbs significant costs. As product life cycles become shorter, but research and development become longer, costs of technology, transfer of technology, and obsolescence become cost drivers. Life-cycle costing addresses this changing environment. Japanese companies have become particularly adept at the life-cycle accounting application.

Through-put accounting concerns allocation of scarce resources and improving the material allocation within the manufacturing process. It is beginning to overtake the traditional way of calculating profitability on the basis of contribution margins. Most manufacturing processes have bottlenecks which impact heavily on the ability of the plant to alter the speed and volume of production. By explicit attention to the production flows and bottleneck back-ups, costs are adjusted for the utilization of the bottleneck process. In this way the profit figures more accurately reflect the real cost of using the scarce resource in production processing.[10]

Auditing TQM Performance

These techniques are highly useful amendments to the traditional managerial accounting performed to achieve enhanced profitability. On the other hand, the U.S. has seen Japan pull ahead in innovation with regard to management. And there is little question that the management accounting data is a critical data component in the quest for the continuous quality improvement sought by TQM advocates. When performance auditing and TQM are linked, we interpret that an independent analysis is present. Reporting the performance audit information with its focus on economy, efficiency, and effectiveness, makes the management adoption of more relevant and reliable costing standards, such as these just outlined, critical to continuous improvement. That is, using performance audit to audit the success of TQM, provides a highly comprehensive and relevant view of the management of an entity. Consider, then, how independent performance audits of TQM companies enhance the credibility of the entity to outsiders, and signal achievement of goals as well to insiders. Performance audit when applied to a TQM organization provides pervasive feed-forward and feed-back data. Figure 4.7 provides a model of this interface.

In TQM, management decisions are made to allocate people and things to products and processes. These decisions are made by teams within the organization, with a view toward achieving customer satisfaction and product/service quality. Within the TQM system a performance measurement system is devised by the team participants to provide evidence of achievements in client satisfaction and movement toward a continuous improvement program. As the performance system reports, teams are empowered to adjust: first, in the allocations of people, things, and processes; second, in the measurement system; and third, in the articulated goals. This continuous loop provides management the flexibility they need to respond to economic, technological, and the entity's resource changes.

In performance audit, independent third parties view the process as inputs (people, things, processes), and outputs (goods and services), and their relationship to the objectives of the entity. By reviewing the achievements with the criteria of economy, efficiency, and effectiveness, an evaluation is possible. This performance audit process provides an independent reporting mechanism to assess what the entity has rendered in terms of "value for money." The performance audit evaluation then becomes informational input into the TQM system as feedback; it also serves as a signaling mechanism to the capital market at large whether the entity is well-run by management.

Figure 4.7
Feed-Forward and Feedback Model of TQM and Performance Audit

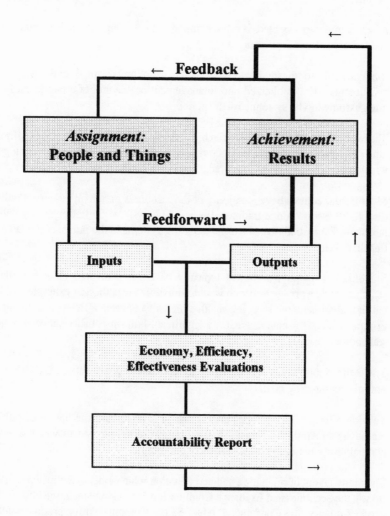

Management Accountability from TQM in the Public Sector

There are unique problems in the implementation of TQM in the public sector, which makes the use of performance audit even more valuable. Among these unique problems are the following:

- In times of economic decline, resources available to public sector entities always decline.

- As government grows there is more competition between state, local, municipal, and federal entities for resources.

- It is difficult to disaggregate government into units which make sense to constituents. The publicized poor management of one unit of a public entity is often assumed to be systemic by the public.

- The focus on the relationship between budgets, expenditures, and variances affords little insight into management effectiveness, as the control variable is the budget, which may not be relevant to sources, needs, allocations, and uses of funds.

- Most public entities have a majority of the resources in human resources rather than fixed assets; since traditional accounting systems do not explicitly value human resources, traditional financial reporting systems in the public sector do not translate well.

- Stakeholders in public entities typically have more diverse objectives than shareholders in a private firm who want to maximize wealth. For example, public entities are often involved in wealth transfers between affluent and indigent groups, which, for many, creates a significant built-in conflict between major stakeholder groups.

- Thus, the public entity has difficulty maximizing a goal; rather, they have to optimize competing goals.

- Service efforts and accomplishments are so diverse, and the nature of public entities is so similarly diverse, that a uniform reporting system which affords comparability between entities is nearly impossible.

- The many layers of regulation and accreditation which exist in the private sector (to wit, the Securities and Exchange Commission for issuing stock, the NSIST for product quality, the Consumer Product Safety Commission for product safety, OSHA for employee safety) do not apply to the public sector.

All of these factors, individually and in combination, mean that accountability reporting provides great benefits to stakeholders. The diversity, complexity, and size of public entities make it difficult for stakeholders to digest public information. In many cases public information is not disseminated well; when is the last time a charitable organization who has made a telephone solicitation during dinnertime disclosed its rate of administrative cost per dollar contributed to you? In most cases information is not disaggregated sufficiently to distinguish between effective management in subunits. Furthermore, in the absence of the residual ownership concept used in the private sector to evaluate enhanced value, there is not a cumulative or comprehensive way in which to compare entities. The "continuous improvement" concept which is so intrinsic to TQM cannot be brought to light over a three-to-five year time horizon.

Performance Measurement Needs Reporting

A comprehensive report[11] was issued by the Committee on Nonprofit Entities' Performance Measures of the American Accounting Association's Government and Nonprofit Section to evaluate possible systems for the implementation of service efforts and accomplishments reporting for various segments of the public sector. They considered health-related organizations, museums and cultural organizations, hospitals, religious entities, and institutions of higher education. Of particular interest to us in investigating the link between TQM and performance auditing is the example of United Way cited in the report.

United Way, beginning in 1972, began to use a comprehensive reporting system for performance which included 587 programs providing 231 services which are collapsed into 33 service systems for eight classifications of service efforts.[12] The system purported to put accountability and continuous performance review into the organization, and offered a uniform reporting system. Unfortunately, the system has not realized accountability.

In fact, several unfortunate scandals involving United Way have surfaced, resulting in decreases in donations to many other organizations. To help deal with the accountability crisis, the Council on Foundations put together a task force to monitor compliance by its members with the group's principles.[13] This came when it was disclosed that outside auditors would be called in after United Way's president, William Aramony, instructed that selected financial records be destroyed in 1992.

In an effort to restore credibility, Elaine Chao, previously running the Peace Corps Program, was brought on as president and CEO of United Way in 1993. She has had to overcome negative information to contributors; it was disclosed variously that the director received from $390,000 to $500,000 per year in salary, but was also compensated by an undisclosed $73,000 in benefits.[14] Furthermore, extensive spending on entertainment, personal expenses, and other perks increase the compensation figure even higher, and ultimately led to lack of confidence and measurably reduced donations to the entity.

Accounting Principles and Accountability

Some research, however, is critical of the attempt to make accountability the cornerstone of promulgated, generally accepted accounting principles. The Governmental Accounting Standards Board has articulated accountability as the overriding criterion in financial reporting of not-for-profit organizations. This objective is particularly difficult to implement in the accounting reports of state and local governments because financial statement users are particularly diverse, and have competing cost/benefit objectives in seeking certain data from a public entity.[15] In the federal government in particular, significant use of inflexible centralization, unnecessary layers of management review, and burdensome paperwork prevail. In effect, unless TQM is adopted by most federal entities in one agency, it is likely to be ineffectual in a few. The historical philosophy and prevailing management techniques, the need to cut the labor force, and the requirements of integrating information with so vast a number of other intra- and inter- subagency offices makes piecemeal implementation of TQM nearly meaningless.

Obstacles to TQM Favor Performance Audit

Saturation of a TQM philosophy in public management encounters other significant obstacles as well. Management's unwillingness to be flexible in its particular environment is often a problem.[16] For example, again using the federal government as a case analysis, consider the unavoidable differences in the workforces of different federal or quasi-federal entities. The Securities and Exchange Commission is dominated by highly educated workers, while the U.S. Post Office employs, on the whole, skilled, but less educated workers.

The SEC workers are not in positions where redundancy in task is the rule, and easy exchangeability of workers is rarely achieved. On the other hand, the U.S. Post Office has a work force in which it is able to train large numbers of personnel to achieve highly similar work tasks. Effectiveness is more easily measured, performance is more easily quantified, and transferability of workers is more realizable in the latter agency. In addition, there is a high level of agreement among interest groups on the goals and objectives of the latter agency, while interest groups in the operations of the SEC have more diverse interests and must lobby for dominance.

Furthermore, because of the lower level of complexity in assessing satisfaction with services provided by the U.S. Post Office as opposed to the S.E.C., management reporting of operations is simplified in the Post Office case. Thus, a clearly reported and widely disseminated performance audit of the Post Office alone, even without a TQM implementation, is likely to have pervasive impact on the operation of the entity. Reporting in the case of the SEC is a beneficial but less clear activity, since operations are diverse, and interest group demands for information compete with each other and are complex.

Environmental Impediments to TQM

In order to implement TQM, employees must be able to assess the responsibility for work assignments and also understand where their decision-making begins and ends. Sometimes, to foster this environment, work teams rather than individuals define the tasks and decision responsibilities. But in any case, organizations with more complex responsibilities, more diverse work assignments, and less congruence of goals will encounter a more challenging assignment in adopting TQM. With respect to government operations, a particularly daunting requirement is to provide information which will affect taxpayer opinion and perception.

Some federal entities have experimented with other management systems in order to achieve more seamless operations and better accountability. For example, the U.S. Office of Personnel Management has adopted many different human resource management system paradigms in the last fifteen years on an experimental basis.[17]

Take, for example, one of President Clinton's prime concerns with health care spending on the part of individuals outside of the federal government. He has proposed caps on the increases in health insurance premium costs. Essentially, these are price controls reminiscent of the wage and price controls advocated by President Jimmy Carter as a mechanism to deal with the aberrantly high inflation rates experienced during his administration. But price and cost controls which are mandated often fly directly against the need for accountability and TQM.

Implementation of cost controls costs real money. Furthermore, cost control does not assure or encourage quality. Also, cost controls do little or nothing to foster consumer satisfaction or measure effectiveness of services provided. The Jackson Hole Group which looked at health care cost containment proposed a far more modern and forward-thinking plan; that is, to implement cost and quality controls not by executive fiat, but by providing sufficient information to customers and relying on them to make use of competition by evaluating satisfaction with patient care on both dimensions of cost and quality. Customers want both lower costs and higher quality of services. Those health-care groups which are able to optimize these sometimes competing objectives will receive more client groups. Thus, there is a built-in incentive for improvement on the part of the health-care groups, as opposed to an externally mandated cost cap which neither addresses accountability nor quality.

Performance Audit Represents Stability

This is why many professionals have been reluctant to embrace TQM for the public sector, while retaining confidence in performance auditing. In evaluating the report card of TQM in the public sector, one cognoscenti notes, "The spectrum of opinion on TQM applications in government agencies presently stretches from exaggerated claims regarding its universal applicability and potency to more agnostic reservations related to its unspecified or undeveloped theoretical linkages to outright dismissals . . . in the fact of organizations realpolitik."[18] To forward TQM goals the author suggests a contingency theory approach to TQM in government applications.

But the fact remains that the report card is still largely unknown for entities in the public sector in their experiences with TQM. Uneven applications, lack of public reporting on results, and resistance among traditional managers in a governmental setting have not supported a comprehensive analysis of TQM effectiveness.

Another reason for the absence of evaluation of the results of public sector TQM relates to the lack of an appropriate model of assessment. Several models have been proposed which are purportedly applicable to the public sector. These include a generalistic model of causality, a two-factor model, and a stage/state model.[19] The two-factor model operates by defining a relevant operation, measuring it, and using TQM as the intervening variable which affects it. In this way it is at least theoretically possible to measure the effect of TQM. The stage/state model considers teams of workers going through stages of implementation of TQM and proceeds to measure the state of change at each stage. In any case an appropriate model of evaluation for TQM in the public sector is performance auditing itself. Performance variables are identified and analyzed for economy, efficiency, and effectiveness. In the federal government, even with the implementation of the Chief Financial Officers Act, supported by agency Inspector Generals, no such widespread study has been undertaken. But performance auditing results are becoming increasingly public in the quest for accountability.

Is Continuous Improvement Realistic? The Private Sector Experiment

James Riles, as senior vice president of the Juran Institute, has asserted that TQM, in addressing continuous improvement of organizations, does affect profits and company market share by zeroing in on product improvement and product responsiveness.[20] The *Wall Street Journal* has reported that the success rate of TQM in the private sector is limited, because companies lack experience and appropriate training. In addition, a survey revealed the 945 different TQM strategies were employed in 584 companies,[21] leading one to recognize that implementation is highly individualistic and based on trial and error. More specifically, the ISO 9000 requirements for quality standards are particularly appropriate for TQM in the private sector, because the measurement system is already derived, and the performance standards are specified in the regulations.

The Public Sector Experiment

The President's Council on Integrity and Efficiency (PCIE) reports on investigations in the federal sector which pertain to audit findings and management performance. For example, audits located nearly fifty thousand inappropriate claims in 1991 in Veterans Affairs at an unnecessary cost of nearly $700 million. In response, the VA instituted quality training programs, increased internal controls, new information systems, and reallocated personnel.[22]

The National Performance Review issued a report, "Improving Financial Mismanagement" in 1993 which describes 13 areas where federal financial management could be improved. It was assisted by the Coalition for Effective Change which was made up of nearly thirty organizations with a stake in improving federal management. It is ironic that in calling for more effective financial controls and reporting, the NPR targets accountants (suggesting cuts of 700,000 control positions) and proposing to cut in half the ratio of managers and supervisors to employees in the next five years.[23] These changes are taking place in defiance of the Governmental Accounting Standards Board, which has jurisdiction over state, local, municipal, and other nonprofit entities. GASB has issued Statement 14, The Financial Reporting Entity. In this document, accountability relationships are explored which are to be used in deciding which units to "consolidate" into a reporting entity. The proliferation of reporting under this standard is sure to be considered by the comparable federal group charged with promulgating standards for the federal bureaucracy.

Performance Audit is Needed to Supplement TQM for External Accountability

There are occasional heart-warming stories about integrity in government and highly professional behavior in government. For example, Carol Browner, the chief administration officer of the Environmental Protection Agency, gets consistently good marks for using the agency to get the most out of the mutual goals of government and business.[24] In addition, Hazel O'Leary, who heads up the Department of Energy, has been noted for her willingness to reinvent government through the use of Total Quality Management.[25] In an editorial a journalist praised the Department of the Navy for its straightforward response to his request for information. The Department willingly provided the data relating to Navy pilots who received credit for flight time when they went to New Orleans to Mardi Gras.[26] And in an honest moment, a County Executive in Milwaukee, Wisconsin, encouraged his Board of Supervisors to send funds back to the federal government. They had been given funds to set up a substance abuse treatment center specifically for area residents who turned to drugs and alcohol due to anxiety about the flooding in the Midwestern area in 1993. They did not accept the funds for a simple reason: their community was never flooded.[27]

More common are stories of government waste, fraud, and inefficiency. A General Accounting Office Report disclosed that the Jet Propulsion Laboratory of NASA has allowed thousands of dollars of assets to walk home with employees after work, including government property such as PCs, fax equipment, and portable phones.[28] Grant funds were extended to the National Cattleman's Association by the Environmental Protection Agency in the amount of half a million dollars. The grant's purpose was to analyze the burps of cows for methane emissions. The Association noted with sarcasm that cattle burps are an extremely negligible source of methane.[29] A group called Citizens Against Government Waste was less concerned with cattle than pigs. It issued a 1994 Congressional Pig Summary which it characterized as a "veritable pu-pu platter of pork" including examples of funding it considers unworthy to the tune of $1.2 billion.[30] Furthermore, it appears that the medical school of the federal government, the Uniformed Services University of the Health Sciences, which was formed to supply the military with doctors, needs to be closed. Estimates of savings run as high as $300 million over five years if the school, which costs five times as much to train a physician as a state or private university, were closed.[31] Also, advisory boards to the federal government, at an estimated $17 million per year, were taken to task. With nearly three hundred such boards, including a Board of Tea Experts, which are authorized by law, few discernable benefits have been recognized.

Some projects are even more dramatic in their wastefulness. In one particularly disturbing case, ten mentally retarded patients were warehoused in substandard housing with poor living conditions and inadequate food and clothing in Queens, New York. The combined tab for the ten patients contributed by both the state and federal programs was $2 million for a four-year period, or $50,000 per patient per year. In addition to that cost the individual in charge of the patients embezzled another half million.[32] While the military is struggling with budget constraints involving both physical and human resources, personnel at the Pentagon were using a rather expensive rapid transit method. It is fourteen miles between Andrews Air Force Base and the Pentagon. But instead of the mundane method of automobile, Pentagon personnel logged in nearly two hundred and fifty helicopter jaunts from the Pentagon to Andrews AFB. Each trip costs upwards of three thousand dollars as opposed to $15 to $25 for a car.[33] Those who proposed and passed original legislation to stockpile helium because of a predicted temporary shortage had good intentions. They will be horrified to learn that the Bureau of Mines has continued to acquire helium since 1960 in a storage facility even though during the last three and a half decades, there has never been a shortage, and the predicted shortage in 1960 did not occur. The cost to taxpayers is around $1.3 billion.[34]

All of these disturbing lapses in spending tax dollars to serve constituents have occurred in spite of the fact that the General Accounting Office boasts that two-thirds of the nearly three thousand separate units of the federal government are engaged in total quality management.[35] Local governments profess to have found the key as well with TQM. In Detroit, Mayor Dennis Archer is an advocate of TQM to solve the considerable and long-standing problems of the urban environment. Prince George's County, Maryland has converted to TQM.[36] And Palatine, Illinois, feels that TQM will make "the taxpayer king" and improve services across all applications.[37] Cities like Philadelphia, Indianapolis, and Boston have implemented purported programs to measure performance.[38]

Vice President Al Gore, operating through a National Performance Review which made recommendations to President Clinton, held a summit on Reinventing Government. At the conference, the Vice President repeatedly advocated a TQM approach throughout the federal bureaucracy beginning in 1993. But skepticism abounds. Some current estimates of waste and fraud in federal operations run as high as 25 percent of the total budget.[39] Another author alleges that $300 billion has been lost in the federal government in four years, due to waste and fraud.[40] Such massive efforts are a response to the public's disenchantment with government services. One poll which tapped consumer's feelings alleged that the need to improve government efficiency was a high priority.[41]

TQM, while useful and relevant in many applications, is highly systems-oriented rather than looking from the outside in a stewardship function. In fact, some other methods such as the critical event model work relatively well in training personnel to achieve objectives and improve productivity.[42] This model explicitly takes strategic objectives and applies a model of performance consequences which encourages innovation and problem solving. The use of TQM is most certainly going to have some positive effects on any organization, even federal entities. But waste, fraud, misuse of assets, and program failures are not the focus of TQM. Customer satisfaction and streamlined services are the focus. Performance audit adds to this scenario a reporting function to the public which provides confidence in a broad range of stewardship functions of management. Whether in the public sector or the private, waste, fraud, and inefficiency need to be reduced to levels which maintain the confidence of taxpayers and capital providers. Accountability is enhanced by TQM, but indices of economy, efficiency, and effectiveness reported to the public have been highly regarded in the quest for external validity.

NOTES

1. The following is a particularly lucid article on this subject. Robert M. Grant, Rami Shani, and R. Krishnan. "TQM's Challenge to Management Theory and Practice." *Sloan Management Review* 35:2 (Winter 1994): 25–35.

2. Anne M. Porter. "Baldrige Winners Discuss Continuous Improvement Path." *Purchasing* 11:4 (January 14, 1993): 55–58.

3. Auditing Concepts Committee. "Report of the Committee on Basic Auditing Concepts." *The Accounting Review* 47 (Supplement 1972): 18.

4. John R. Dew. "Measuring Total Quality Management." *Tapping the Network Journal* 5:1 (Spring, 1994): 6–9.

5. Paul Carson and Kerry D. Carson. "Deming versus Traditional Management Theorists on Goal Setting: Can Both Be Right?" *Business Horizons* 3:5 (Sept./Oct. 1993): 79–84.

6. Carson and Carson. 1993.

7. Armand Feigenbaum. "Linking Quality Processes to International Leadership." In *Making Total Quality Happen: Research Report No. 937*. Frank Caropreso, ed. New York: Conference Board. 1990. pp. 3–6.

8. P. Anne Van't Haaff. "Total Quality in the European Environment." In *Making Total Quality Happen: Research Report No. 937*. Frank Caropreso, ed. New York: The Conference Board. 1990. p. 11.

9. While there are more recent works on this subject, this work is comprehensive on this subject. Brian Maskell. *Performance Measurement for World Class Manufacturing: A Model of American Companies*. Cambridge, MA: Productivity Press. 1991. p. 366.

10. Eliyahu Goldratt and Jeff Cox. *The Goal*. Croton-on-Hudson, New York: North River Press. 1984.

11. Committee on Nonprofit Entities' Performance Measures, American Accounting Association Government and Nonprofit Section. *Measuring the Performance of Nonprofit Organizations: The State of the Art*. Sarasota, FL: American Accounting Association. 1989.

12. Committee on Nonprofit Entities' Performance Measures. 1989.

13. "Business Bulletin: Under Scrutiny." *The Wall Street Journal* May 5, 1994, A:1:5.

14. "A Charitable Salary." *The Washington Post* February 20, 1992, A:24:1.

15. James M. Patton. "Accountability and Governmental Financial Reporting." *Financial Accountability and Management* 8:3 (Autumn 1992): 165–180.

16. Beryl A. Radin and Joseph N. Coffee. *Public Administration Quarterly* 17:1 (Spring 1993): 42–54.

17. Brigitte W. Schay. "In Search of the Holy Grail: Lessons in Performance Management." *Public Personnel Management* 22:4 (Winter 1993): 649–68.

18. Robert F. Durant and Laura A. Wilson. "Public Management, TQM, and Quality Improvement: Toward a Contingency Strategy." *American Review of Public Administration* 23:3 (September 1993): 215–45.

19. Laura A. Wilson. "Evaluating Total Quality Management: The Case for a Theory Driven Approach." *Public Administration Review* 5:2 (March/April 1994): 137–46.

20. Shari Caudron. "Just Exactly What is Total Quality Management?" *Personnel Journal* 72:2 (February 1993): 32.

21. Shari Caudron. "Keys to Starting A TQM Program." *Personnel Journal* 72:2 (February 1993): 28–35.

22. Frontline. *Newsletter of the President's Council for Integrity and Efficiency.* (December 1991): 12.

23. Dwight R. Foster. "AGA Joins Coalition to Influence National Performance Review." *Topics* (August 1994): 11.

24. "A Blueprint for Better Government." *Chicago Tribune* August 8, 1994, 1:12: 1.

25. Joel Garreau. "Quality Path Beckons as Reinventing Government Progresses." *The Washington Post* November 3, 1993, A:25:1.

26. Gregg Thomas. "A Salute to the Navy's Openness." *Times-Picayune* January 30, 1994, B:1:7.

27. "Asides: A Profile in Honesty." *The Wall Street Journal* July 22, 1994, A:1:1.

28. Robert Lee Hotz. "A Black Hole for JPL Property." *Los Angeles Times* May 11, 1994, B:1:1.

29. Greg Ruehle. "Belching Cattle." *Chicago Tribune* July 3, 1994, 4:4:2.

30. Rosalind Jackler. "Citizens Group Squeals on Pork-barrel Projects." *The Houston Post* February 17, 1994, A:2:1.

31. Sabra Chartrand. "Pentagon's Medical School May be Mustered Out." *New York Times* September 29, 1993, B:1:7.

32. Selwyn Raab. "Abuse Found in Center for Retarded." *The New York Times* July 7, 1994, B:1:4.

33. John Lancaster. "Defense Brass Flying High—But Not Far." *The Washington Post* May 1, 1994, A:1:1.

34. "Asides: A Hot Air Surplus." *The Wall Street Journal* August 25, 1994, A:1:12.

35. John Hillkirk. "Uncle Sam Begins Push for Quality." *USA Today* October 7, 1992, B:5:1.

36. Leonard Hughes. "A New Strategy Emerges for Front-Line Workers." *The Washington Post* January 14, 1993, MDP:2:1.

37. "Teresa Wiltz. Palatine's New Credo: The Taxpayer's Always Right." *Chicago Tribune* May 31, 1992, 2NW:1:1.

38. Adrian Walker. "Boston's Budget to be Performance-Based." *Boston Globe* April 18, 1994, 3:15.

39. John Hillkirk. "Clinton Plans Moves Away from Waste." *USA Today* February 25, 1993, B:4:1.

40. "Smart Spending." *Houston Chronicle* February 1, 1993, A:1:12.

41. Richard Benedetto. "Poll: People Want Government to Work, Period." *USA Today* September 16, 1993, A:3:1.

42. Blue Wooldridge. "Increasing the Productivity of Public-Sector Training." *Public Productivity Review* XII:2 (Winter 1988): 205–17.

Chapter 5

The International Development
of Performance Auditing

INTRODUCTION

In order to control costs and become more responsive to citizen and legislative concern with the allocation of increasingly scarce public resources, a growing number of nations have enacted standards for the implementation of performance audit. A wide variety of governments have defined narrow circumstances under which performance audits should be practiced, while other nations call for comprehensive utilization of performance audit. This chapter investigates the development of performance audit in a multinational context. First, the substantial differences in the practices of public performance audits among nations are examined. Then, the chapter develops a performance audit model for multinational corporations in the private sector.

PUBLIC SECTOR APPLICATIONS

The multinational development of standards by enactment of legislation has increased dramatically in recent years. However, both in nations with standards and without, the scope of the performance audit varies considerably, and a scope comparison is presented in this chapter, revealing the differences in breadth. Concomitant with the variation in scope, reporting practices on the results of the performance audits have differed between nations. These reporting differences are examined in the chapter. Subsequent discussion brings focus to a common problem in performance auditing which is handled differently in different nations. This problem relates to the difficulty in staffing the performance audit due to the breadth of professional experience required to undertake the comprehensive audit. Finally, there is evidence of a changing public awareness of and concern for the efficiency of public governance; this has led to an evolving demand for a change in reporting. The new reporting is moving towards an enhanced "social contract" between the public and public managers. This evolving concept of social contract further indicates an increased demand for the widespread development of the practice of performance audits.

COMMON OBJECTIVES OF PERFORMANCE AUDIT
ACROSS NATIONS

As many nations experience increasing demand for public goods and services, they also report shrinking tax bases and strong competition between public constituencies for the allocation of public money. Furthermore, many private international financing institutions have grown skittish about providing funds where the host nation cannot assure adequate internal control or provide reliable reporting mechanisms. Also, the burgeoning foreign debt crisis among developing nations has led to the demand for better accountability from both citizens and financing organizations. In rare instances, such as the Australian Audit Office, a step beyond traditional performance audit is practiced; in Australia, not only are performance audits provided, but, in addition, program effectiveness reviews are accomplished which analyze the effectiveness of policy itself.[1]

Performance audits may be required by statute, they may occur at the discretion of an auditor general, or they may take place due to the insistence of an external financing agency. The report may be provided only to the affected management, or it may be required to go to the legislature. Some reports are confidential, while others are in the public domain. In some cases, the auditors are independent, in others, not. Many nations have their auditor general offices both set standards and use the standards they have themselves promulgated.

Performance audit has achieved wide reaching changes at the municipal, state or province, and national level in many applications. In Portland, Oregon, performance audits have recognized cumulatively over six million dollars in savings, from such roles as city risk management, employee health benefit cost containment, and delinquent assessment identification.[2] In Canada, performance audits are pervasively performed at the federal, provincial, municipal, and Crown Corporation level. In the Philippines, insolvency ensued when a crushing external debt provided minimal assistance to the public because poor internal control led to wasteful and inappropriate disbursement of funds. In Japan, it was found through performance audit that the nation was importing medical equipment rather than buying it internally, because the procurement system did not take into consideration the rising value of the yen against the dollar.[3] In the United States, The Department of Health and Human Services, which under Public Law 94-505 appointed an independent Inspector General for the first time in the federal government, utilized the performance audit concept to, in the Inspector General's words, "become the agent for positive change."[4] As part of this environment of change the Department instituted a system designated as Service Delivery Assessment. This system evaluates programs without using existing, possibly inappropriate, measures of performance.[5] In one reported performance audit, the benefit/cost return was $3.50 for each audit dollar.[6]

PROMULGATION OF STANDARDS FOR PERFORMANCE AUDIT IN DIFFERENT NATIONS

With the call for improved accountability an increasing number of nations have promulgated standards for the practice of performance audits. In many cases these standards are enacted through the legislature, several times under pressure from those offices charged with the maintenance of internal control standards. In these instances auditors have encouraged the development of performance audit because it leads to a more integrated system of internal control, and more relevant reporting. In other cases the enactment of standards was instigated by political interests, for the purpose of making better allocation decisions, and having better feedback information on expenditures. In still other countries there are no national standards. Yet private financial institutions providing private placement of capital, or quasiprivate institutions such as the World Bank or the United Nations, have made performance audit a precondition for loans for infrastructure development. In such countries, performance audits are sporadic and typically triggered by external authorities rather than internal initiatives. In still other countries, shortages of professional or skilled workers exist, and performance audits, if mandated by statute, would be difficult or extremely expensive to perform. In these instances, while there may be a need for performance audit which is supported by the public sector, the only way in which the audit can take place is if the private sector becomes more involved. Even so, the expense may make the performance audit untenable. The following discussion, then, is broken into four broad categories of national groups: well-defined standards with statutory authority, defined standards without statutory authority, loosely defined standards with statutory authority, and special project applications by extranational authority.

Western Nations and Japan

The western nations, particularly Canada, the United Kingdom, and Australia tend to have well-defined performance standards, including delineation of the audit scope, audit practices, and reporting requirements. New Zealand also falls into this category. Japan in addition has substantial experience with performance audit and is discussed in this section. These nations use performance audit pervasively throughout their governmental operations.

In the United States the standards are set by the public sector, for the public sector, meaning that the performance audits are the result of self-regulation. Furthermore, the United States has not legislated standards per se; i.e., the audits are not the result of Congressional authority. One expert finds that the role of the General Accounting Office [GAO] is an anathema to independence, noting that "in other countries, government audit departments would not be allowed to audit self-imposed standards."[7] In the United States the GAO is charged with promulgation of accounting systems and standards for federal agencies. A recent revision of the Yellow Book calls for increased surveillance of federal expenditures and control system review to ensure efficiency within the federal sector. Included in the revision is an expansion of the role outlined in the Yellow Book as far back as 1972; in that publication, "Standards for Audit of Government Organizations, Programs, Activities and Functions," operational audits, compliance audits, and audits of economy, efficiency, and effectiveness were mentioned. Subsequently, in 1978, the GAO put out "Comprehensive Approach for Planning and Conducting a Program Results Review" which again addressed the economy, efficiency, and effectiveness criteria for audit. Thus, the Comptroller General of the United States is charged with implementation of the GAO standards on performance auditing.

In the private sector there are some standards in the United States. The *American Institute of Certified Public Accountants; Statements on Auditing Standards Number 30* is relevant to performance. In particular, it addresses the responsibility of external auditors to review internal control for purposes other than the traditional financial reports. External auditors may express an opinion on internal control for the purpose of "special purpose reports" which may be construed to include the performance audit.[8]

In the Australian Audit Office, performance audits have been done since the 1970s. The initial impetus was the 1974 Royal Commission on Government Administration. The AAO was provided with standards by an amendment in 1979 to the Audit Act, where the audits were termed "efficiency" rather than value-for-money audits. In Australia a distinction is drawn between performance audits, which review managerial effectiveness, and program effectiveness review, which has as its focus a review of government policies.[9] The Australian Auditor General set up an Efficiency Audit Division in 1979, which has since been abolished; The Department of Prime Minister was then given performance audit authority. Furthermore, some dissension exists regarding the appropriate administration of performance audit. There is evidence that political sensitivity has led to differential administration of Australian performance audit, with Queensland and South Australian Auditor Generals performing all type of audits, while Victoria's Auditor General follows the Canadian model.[10]

In Canada, a 1977 Auditor General Act formally legislated performance audit, which was implemented in provincial governments (Prince Edward Island, Ontario, British Columbia, and Alberta). At that time, the Crown Corporations were not included in the performance concept. They were brought into the scheme by Bill C-24, promulgated in 1984, which gave Crown Corporation directors responsibility for economy, efficiency, and effectiveness within their organizations. Bill C-24 was comprehensive, mandating an audit opinion on managerial performance in the area of effectiveness, efficiency, and economy. Bill C-90, legislated in 1984, gave Quebec's Auditor General the mandate to execute performance audits. Further implementation of performance audit has been made possible by a performance audit guide for provinces.[11] An extensive guide was published for cities.[12]

In the United Kingdom, the 1983 National Audit Act mandated performance audits to be performed by the Comptroller and Auditor General in the National Audit Office. The Local Government Finance Act of 1982 mandated performance evaluation for local government in England and Wales.[13] Performance audit is both more recent and more comprehensive in England than in the United States or Canada. Several authors attribute its initiation to the beginning of the Conservative Party administration in 1979.[14] An Audit Commission was set up in 1983, concurrent with the National Audit Act, which specified performance auditing by 1984.

In New Zealand there was a governmental scandal and widespread dissatisfaction with the inefficiency and lack of accountability of government. In addition there was a desire to use zero base budgeting to restrain the growth of public spending. This led to performance audit standards.[15] The Public Finance Act of 1977 set up an independent audit agency with an auditor general. This office has set up its program based on the acronym CARE. This is discussed below under the comparative analysis of procedures which follows this section. It has been noted that New Zealand has had difficulty fulfilling its performance mission because productivity measures have not been developed sufficiently.[16]

Japan has a long history of public audit. Both disclosure rules and audit expectations are advanced. The Board of Audit initiated governmental audits in 1880.[17] However, until recent years, the primary emphasis has been on compliance auditing rather than performance auditing. The Annual Audit Report by the Board of Audit has placed an increasing priority on efficiency, effectiveness, and economy audits by reporting on abuses, frauds, and expenditures with low social returns. This has given the public a developing awareness of the need for pervasive performance auditing.

A President of the Board of Audit, Keiichi Tsuji, refers to two types of audits performed in Japan: micro and macroaudit.[18] The essential characteristics of the microaudit are a search for compliance, fraud, and misappropriation. In the case of the microaudit, the results are presented to the management of the audited unit to provide an opportunity for demonstration of improvement prior to a write-up in the Annual Audit Report.

On the other hand, the macroaudit is similar to a performance audit in that it takes a close look at the achievement of policy objectives rather than examining internal control weakness. Typically, the results of the performance audit are not discussed with management of the audit unit prior to presentation in the Annual Audit Report. Furthermore, while the microaudit calls for immediate improvement in deficiencies found by the audit, the macroaudit calls for an audit opinion and a public disclosure of need for systemic improvement.

Tsuji further reports on the concept of social audit, which, again, is similar to a traditional performance audit. In the social audit the audit team is examining the degree of success in fulfilling the nation's social needs as provided by the public sector. The distinguishing characteristic between the macroaudit and the social audit is that the macroaudit includes an examination of fixed assets and capital expenditures such as road, school, or hospital construction, while the social audit objective is transfer payments for social welfare, i.e., intangible assets or cash disbursement expenditures without immediate tangible results. Japan's performance concept, then, is similar to that of the western nations, but is broken down into more discrete categories.

Other International Initiatives

Some general standardized initiatives have been made by three organizations: the International Organization of Supreme Audit Institutions [INTOSAI], the Asian Organization of Supreme Audit Institutions [AOSAI], and the United Nations. INTOSAI produced the Declaration of Lima in 1983, which supported both the financial and the performance audit concepts. This was supplemented by the AOSAI's 1985 Tokyo Declaration of Guidelines on Public Accountability. Again, the performance audit concept was supported. A subsequent INTOSAI conference in 1985 was specifically on the topic of performance audit. Finally, the United Nations produced the *Handbook on Government Auditing in Developing Countries*. The United Nations document presents some confusion between financial and performance auditing.[19] Clearly, the reduction of trade barriers under treaties such as General Agreement on Tariffs and Trade (GATT), has also provided opportunities and demand for enhanced reporting and auditing of performance data. There is some thought that treaties such as GATT will also further the demand for harmonization of international standards.[20]

Developing Nations: China, Mexico, St. Lucia, and Pakistan

There have been several developing nations which have enacted standards, but in which the procedures and scope of the performance audit function is still limited. These nations include China, Mexico, St. Lucia, and Pakistan. In China an unusual extension of the performance concept is present. A new opportunity for widespread public audit was initiated by the adoption of a new constitution in China in 1982. This constitution mandated a new Audit Administration with an auditor general at the helm to audit revenues and expenses of the State Council. By 1983, the Chinese State Audit Administration was supplemented by many provincial and municipal audit segments.[21] A possibly unexpected facet of the Chinese Audit Administration is its independence; the Constitution provides that the Auditor General is appointed and dismissed by the recommendation of the Premier, and his appointment is voted upon by the National People's Congress for ratification. In China, like the United States, the Audit Administration is charged with both the promulgation of standards and the performance of the audit, in compliance with the audit standards it set for itself. It is not clear at this time that specific standards have been promulgated for separate performance audits.

In Mexico a mandate was given to the auditor general to "help make federal government more honest, efficient, effective, responsive, transparent, and accountable."[22] In an interesting division of duties the auditor general is responsible for performance auditing in the federal agencies, federal districts, and state agencies. However, the practice of auditing is by the auditor general's staff in the federal sector, while most state agency audits are performed by private external auditors. But the responsibility for the state audit remains with the auditor general. The external auditors are appointed by the auditor general's office.

St. Lucia adopted Program Planning and Budgeting Systems (PPBS) in the 1980s. This provided an impetus to initiate performance auditing for feedback purposes. With the requested assistance, in 1983, of the Canadian International Development Agency, an auditor general's office was set up in 1985 and was operational by 1986. The office was strengthened by a 1987 Auditor General Act to St. Lucia's Parliament to assure independence of the agency and its officers, and to empower them to audit pervasively.[23] The expertise of Canada, as well as that of private sector auditors, has been essential to the initiatives of St. Lucia.

In Pakistan, an Office of the Auditor General has undertaken the accomplishment of performance audit since 1978. The original mandate was for the efficiency audit of public enterprise, but this was expanded in 1981 to government agencies as well.[24] While the mandate is for the extensive use of performance audit, the promulgation of standards and the unavailability of auditors who are experienced in performance procedures has impeded the widespread implementation of performance audit in Pakistan.

Special Use Nations: Malaysia, the Philippines, Thailand, and Cyprus

The final category of countries includes those who use performance auditing for special purposes, primarily capital projects. In most cases the initiative for the performance audit is from an agency external to the nation, such as the World Bank or the United Nations. These nations include Malaysia, the Philippines, Thailand, and Cyprus.

In Cyprus, an office of audits under an Auditor General has been operational since the 1970s, but only since the 1980s has this office engaged itself in performance audits. The need for performance auditing derived from the high proportion of the Cypriot budget which is designated for capital asset projects. This proportion runs nearly one quarter of national expenses.[25] In the case of Cyprus, the lack of international procedures and lack of experienced personnel has impeded the progress of performance auditing. Therefore, in Cyprus, the performance audit tends to parallel the stages of the capital development project itself, including a review of the economy, efficiency, and effectiveness of the bids from contractors. In cases such as this, the existence of the Auditor General's policy to undertake performance auditing may act as a stimulus to strong internal control and adequate reporting processes. However, there is some concern that the approach to performance audit may be ad hoc.

In Malaysia, the Philippines, and Thailand, the performance audit process has been fostered by the Asian Organization of Supreme Audit Institutions [AOSAI]. In Malaysia, external agencies such as the International Monetary Fund, the Asian Development Bank, The Bank Negara, and the Treasury Department have demanded that performance audit be initiated on their behalf. The primary emphasis of the performance audit is for foreign loans and internal financing by the Department of the Treasury. At the triennial conference of the AOSAI, performance audit experiences were shared toward an objective of improving procedure, reporting, and identification of opportunities in performance auditing.[26]

In the Philippines, a Commission on Audit is empowered to perform effectiveness audits for capital projects financed externally, as well as for evaluation of government debt from external sources. At this time multiple agencies are involved in the operation of performance audit, and there is some evidence that the emphasis is more on compliance than effectiveness.[27] In Thailand, an Office of the Auditor General performs performance audit, which is mandated for federal offices and public enterprises. The emphasis stated in the objectives of the Auditor General's office appears to be more geared toward government solvency and allocation problems than toward efficiency of the public bureaucracy as a whole. Again, foreign loans are singled out for special consideration, and resource problems in obtaining experienced performance auditors appear to be at fault for the inability to manage performance audit on a widespread basis.[28]

SCOPE AND REPORTING DIFFERENCES

Scope, procedure, and reporting depth are varied among nations. Scope refers to the objective of the audit; in comprehensive performance auditing the scope includes the financial audit, the compliance audit, and the operational audit. Procedure refers to the standards for the planning, implementation, and oversight of the audit. Reporting characteristics include both what is reported, as well as to whom it is reported. Some observations and distinctions are discussed below.

In Japan, the United States, Canada, New Zealand, and Australia, the scope of and procedures for performance audits are similar. However, some differences exist. In Japan, economy audits and efficiency audits are conducted and reported on separately. A president of the Board of Audit of Japan explains the difference: in the economy audit, it is asked whether the "government projects could have achieved the same level of performance at a lower cost," while in the efficiency audit, the question is "whether they could have achieved a higher level of performance at the same cost."[29] In the United Kingdom the scope of the audit is extensive; included are consideration of alternatives, conflicts in policy, appropriateness of scale of programs, assumptions made in making allocations, and quality of preparing productivity measures to evaluate policy objectives.[30] The reporting of performance audit results is specified, and it is provided that management should have the opportunity to examine the audit report and prepare a statement of management objectives. In addition, all significant findings are to be reported, including material weaknesses and opportunities for improving efficiency, effectiveness, and economy.

In China, the Audit Administration is charged with investigations of waste and losses, audits where external funds are involved, and "supervision through auditing" of capital projects, budgets, credit agencies, insurance agencies.[31] In an unusual procedural requirement, factory managers are not permitted to retire or change jobs until an audit of their section is conducted. In Australia, New South Wales has performance audits performed by the merit protection agency, rather than the auditor general. Furthermore, confidentiality of performance audits is assured and they do not enter the public domain.[32]

In St. Lucia, the scope includes monetary, human, and physical assets, and reporting on accountability relationships is to be maintained.[33] Canada, from which the St. Lucian model was adopted, also includes human resources, and reporting on the results of the performance audit should include an opinion of economy, efficiency, and effectiveness. In Canada, an extensive array of audit practice guides exists for all levels of government. In the United States, audit practice guides exist, although there is no requirement for a performance audit opinion per se.

SUMMARY OF INTERNATIONAL APPLICATIONS OF PERFORMANCE AUDIT

Across nations there are divergent guidelines for performance audit. These differences include varying scope, reporting, and standards of performance audit. In addition, the confidentiality of reports is sometimes maintained, hampering the public's efforts to assess accountability. In the western nations and Japan, standards for the practice and reporting of performance audit exist, and these audits are implemented pervasively throughout governmental operations. In some nations standards for the practice of performance exist, but reporting and assignment of audit staff may be ad hoc at this time. In yet other nations, performance is practiced only in limited circumstances, and the standards used and reporting practices employed are variable, depending on the requirements of the provider of capital resources.

In most nations a common problem exists. Because of the comprehensive nature of the performance audit, the acquisition of trained audit staff, or the training of existing staff is extremely difficult. In many situations the technical skills needed on one performance audit are not applicable to the next, and either the audit staff must be retrained, or there is a need to have high turnover in the staff. This leads to management and control problems. Furthermore, in many emerging nations, technical deficiencies are such that skilled employees are not available for assignment to performance audits. In these nations the private sector must be called upon to fill the gap, albeit sometimes at a high price. However, employment of private sector auditors may be efficient, because it obviates the need to retrain government staff for each engagement. The private sector public accounting firms are better able to supply the variable expertise required in performance audit in many nations where the technical requirements are high, the engagements variable, and the audit skill of existing staff is limited to financial or compliance audits.

The incidence of performance auditing in the public sector has expanded rapidly. There is clearly an increase in the public demand for information on public management for accountability. Similar to the private sector, financial reporting is changing from a strict stewardship function to an agency contract view. The public is demonstrating a desire to expand the traditional contract between themselves and government. They are demanding information so that they are better able to assess efficiency, economy, and effectiveness from public information themselves, rather than delegating this task to public managers and allowing the public managers to evaluate both managerial and program performance. This is, in essence, a change in the social contract between the public and public managers. There is pressure toward public accountability by informed citizens. Previously, this contract was between citizens and elected officials, wherein public managers were accountable to legislatures or other governing agencies. The existence of performance auditing and reporting has made possible the expanded and more direct accountability of management to citizens. This is, of course, paralleled by the changing environment in financial reporting in the private sector; investors are increasingly demanding information so that they can directly assess the performance of the managers.

A final conclusion rests on the changes needed in the performance environment in the public sector for performance audit to evolve to more nations and for more functions. In order for the evolution to occur, more uniformity among standards for the performance of, and reporting of, performance audits is needed. This may occur by international cooperation, or by the adoption of multinational standards by appropriate multinational governing boards. Such uniformity fosters both better understanding of the results of performance audit as well as research and development into the practice of performance audit.

PERFORMANCE EVALUATION OF MULTINATIONAL FIRMS: PRIVATE SECTOR CONSIDERATIONS

The Unique Challenge of Performance Audit in the International Setting

The needs of capital market participants in the international private sector arena parallel those of participants in a national or public setting. The need to have data and analysis which reports on the stewardship function of management with regard to economy, efficiency, and effectiveness is perhaps even more significant in an environment where cultural, social, and political differences are greater. In addition, the stewardship function is even more critical to evaluate because of the both literal and figurative distance between the home office and the subsidiary in many cases.

There are many organizations involved in the setting of standards, implementation, and disclosure of corporate information, but wide variability in the current environment impedes progress. In fact, research indicates that while some nations have embraced international performance audit reporting standards, many have made the adoption of such standards voluntary, and many have taken no position at all to date.[34] This is understandable in some nations which are still in the process of developing capital market regulation agencies to better handle the needs of equity investors worldwide. In the United States, where highly developed financial reporting standards already exist, a search of the Fortune 500 companies' corporate disclosures found absolutely no reliance or reporting references to the International Accounting Standards Committee (IASC standards).[35] This evidence is corroborated by a *Financial Times* research report which evaluated the top 100 European companies for adherence to IASC standards. The findings indicated a negligible reliance upon IASC pronouncements.[36]

Estimates of organizations in the world today which are advancing this cause toward harmonization of standards run as high as twenty international associations.[37] While the IASC has taken a leadership role in promulgating harmonization of standards, there has been some disenchantment with the level of alternatives in measurement permitted by IASC standards to date. For example, eight of nine measurement standards permit alternative treatments, while those statements which deal with disclosure are more specific and lead to better comparability.[38]

The particular challenges of the multinational environment in the public sector translate into an opportunity and a challenge for auditors. The trend toward mergers and acquisitions and toward increased internationalization of large corporations means that diversity in reporting practices, management styles, rates of returns on assets, and cultural work ethic make traditional financial reports obsolete. More comprehensive information across discipline areas is essential for the management and control of highly diverse operations.

Auditors easily make the case that audits save money, not cost money. By assuring the capital marketplace that there is integrity in financial reports and control within the organization, the assessed risk of the firm is lowered. This results in more capital flowing to the firm, and a lower cost of capital from creditors. Because of enhanced technology, audits are performed more efficiently; also, the information highway permits an ever faster pace of access to information. Finally, because of the ability to access and store vast amounts of information quickly and at little cost, the very nature of reporting is changing. The EDGAR (Electronic Data Gathering and Retrieval) system at the Securities and Exchange Commission ultimately translates into electronic filing by corporations, and electronic retrieval by capital market participants, with no paper and no wait on either side of the transaction. The industry that used to serve us in obtaining annual reports, and for both acquisition of data and dissemination of it, is now obsolete. Instead, these firms are evolving into units which provide more comparative, competitive, and analytical information as their traditional functions dry up.

Furthermore, the point is well made that traditional financial reports reflect less and less well the operating results of the firm. For example, innovations in TQM, just in time inventory management, cycle-time control, and others are neither easily portrayed nor disclosed in annual reports.[39] Electronic data exchange between firms and suppliers, bankers, equity holders, and management means that less data needs to be summarized in reports. Rather, more data is received, and the recipient performs the function of summarization, aggregation, and analysis at the end point of the information exchange. Conceptually, investors are getting less information from annual financial reports (including, of course, quarterlies), and more information from alternative sources. Robert K. Elliott interprets this transformation as an opportunity for the audit profession to respond to the challenge of reconfiguring the information the firm reports and which the auditor reviews.[40]

The current trend toward including nonaudited data in annual reports to shareholders will increase. This is because the disclosures fulfill the needs of capital market participants above and beyond the financial data now reported. As information gains even more complexity in a multinational context, nonaudited data will proliferate and represent new opportunities for analysis. The diversity and intricacy of disclosures in the international context will contribute to a need for assurance of the legitimacy of the disclosure, its freedom from bias, and its timeliness. This is where the multinational performance audit also adds value. The audit adds value by its attest function which provides assurance about the reasonableness and completeness of disclosures. The performance audit adds value by aggregating complex information not disclosed in reports, and providing an evaluation of economy, efficiency, and effectiveness. Particularly in operations which are dispersed geographically, an opportunity to possess assurance about accountability of management to diverse groups of stakeholders is valuable.

Performance evaluation in an international environment is critical to the economic success of the corporate world; in addition, the need to achieve control and drive strategic initiatives smoothly challenges us to expand accountability reporting. In this section a model of accountability reporting for multinational enterprises is developed, along with some discussion of the status of international reporting standards. Of course, limitations of language, currency fluctuations, data quality, and capital market conditions will persist into the twenty-first century. However, in order to meet the needs of users of reports of multinational firms, progress in this area is essential. Without some harmonization and expanded disclosure of management accountability in publicly held multinational corporations, allocation decisions in the global capital market will remain suboptimal.

The Development of International Accounting Standards

The development of international accountability reporting is irretrievably linked with the advancement of international accounting standards in general. The increased harmonization of financial reporting among nations will support uniformity and comparability of accountability information. The record thus far in progressing toward international integration of reporting is equivocal at best, but nevertheless progress is being made.

It is clear that the practice of financial reporting has developed independently in both developed and developing nations. The factors which have influenced the content, amount, and detail of financial reports in different nations have been cultural and related to issues of taxation and government policy. For example, in some nations, equity markets are largely unregulated. In others, while equity markets are regulated, financial disclosure rules are lax or uncodified. In still others, traditional financial audits are not required, which means that capital markets must apply risk analysis to the integrity of financial statements themselves. Thus, accountability is particularly difficult to achieve.

Both economic differences between nations and social influences have affected reporting practices. While there have been ongoing attempts to harmonize accounting standards to enhance comparability of financial reports, progress has been slow.

Research into the effects of country variables on the nature of financial reports has demonstrated that tax policy, country philosophy, capital market sophistication, and management philosophy have determined the direction of reporting in different countries.[41] Reporting practices have followed the evolution of the accounting profession in different countries, and the information needs of the capital market have not been the driving force in forwarding reporting practices. Rather, the growth and development of the practice of public accounting appears to be the overriding criterion in promulgating codified accounting standards.[42]

There is little doubt that the emergence of rapidly developing emerging economies and the growth of the multinational enterprise has led to a resurgence of concern with the development of international accounting standards, internationally consistent reporting standards, and standardization of some kind of regulation of financial markets in the world. The needs of business managers, equity holders, debt holders, and governments need to be fulfilled and harmonization of international business reports will go a long way toward fulfilling these needs. In order for consistent and decision-useful accountability reports to be issued, progress will have to be made in traditional financial reporting.

Cultural relativity theory aside, the IASC has worked tirelessly to promote more standardized reporting mechanisms among nations. There is uniform agreement that the needs of financial statement users will be enhanced by reports which are comprehensive, free from bias, timely, relevant, and verifiable. Furthermore, widespread agreement exists that a key criterion in achieving harmonization will be comprehensiveness of data presented. As standards continue to evolve, the reporting of performance data in the international setting will parallel the development of such reporting in the developed nations. Since England, Australia, New Zealand, and the United States have been forerunners in this initiative, it may be expected that the practices of performance audit in these nations will lead the international development of such standards.

Historically, there have been several international standard-setting organizations. The most influential is the IASC. The IASC issues standards, but is dependent upon other nations to incorporate these standards into the GAAP of the individual nations. This is a voluntary, professional commitment, without the force of law. For example, in the United States, the FASB has to issue its own pronouncement for the IASC standards to take effect. Furthermore, the most troublesome and material differences between reporting standards in different nations, including pension accounting, goodwill, consolidation policy, and financial instrument reporting, bring political considerations into the adoption of international standards. When the United States adopted mark-to-market provisions of short-term debt and equity investments under FASB Standard 115, it meant that balance sheets were enhanced, at least in the short run, by increased current assets. This financial reporting change affects the marketability of U.S. corporate debt and equities in comparison to those of other nations whose balance sheets reflect lower-of-cost-or-market valuation.

The IASC, which was initiated in 1973 by representatives from Germany, France, Australia, Canada, the Netherlands, Ireland, England, Mexico, and Japan, took up the mandate to enhance comparative uniformity between nations' accounting and auditing standards. Its representation now encompasses nearly eighty countries and in excess of one hundred accounting organizations.

Another influential organization is the International Federations of Accountants, which, unlike the IASC, represents accountants as members of a profession, rather than umbrella standard-setting bodies. The IFAC's International Auditing Practices Committee promulgates comparative uniformity among accounting professionals in the way in which audits are conducted. On a rotating basis, the IFAC convenes a World Congress of Accountants, which was last held in Washington, D.C., in conjunction with the International Organization of Supreme Audit Institutes (INTOSAI). INTOSAI takes as its purview the promulgation of audit standards in the public sector.

A very destabilizing influence in the standard-setting environment is presented by the emerging trend toward government involvement in international reporting standards. The Organizations for Economic and Community Development and the United Nations are involved in encouraging member nations to adopt common accounting standards. The acceptance of a formalized agreement of cooperation between countries issued by the U.N. would have to be approved by the legislative branch of government, the U.S. Congress. If Congress becomes involved in the promulgation of accounting standards it will be an entirely radical departure from the system which has been in place since the implementation of the Securities and Exchange Commission in 1934. The SEC has consistently approved delegation of the setting of accounting and auditing standards to the private sector, currently the FASB.

The particular provisions sought by the U.N. and the OECD are enhanced reporting standards. For example, the U.N. had initially produced a document called *Guidelines, 1977,* in which it described the necessary disclosures, both quantitative, and qualitative, that multinational companies should follow. In 1988, the U.N. again voted to promulgate the *Guidelines.* Significantly more information was included in the document than is the current practice in the United States.

The OECD represents primarily fully developed nations as opposed to the many developing nations included in the U.N. It adopted, in 1976, its own format and content for disclosures. However, its influence in actually promulgating standards appears to have taken second place in favor of its focus on encouraging and researching opportunities for harmonization of international accounting standards for the private sector.

In addition, there have been initiatives to enhance uniformity and comparative reporting in various regions of the world. For example, the Confederation of Asian and Pacific Accountants, representing twenty countries in that part of the world, is working toward harmonization of reporting standards in the Pacific Rim. The African Accounting Council, representing 27 nations on that continent, also works toward harmonization. And, in the European Community, EC Directives are the vehicle for standardizing audits and financial reports. Unfortunately, political considerations have impeded the implementation of some Directives, with Italy, for example, adopting in 1992, the Fourth Directive which was issued in 1978.[43] Again, it is necessary to note that the checkered record of amalgamating financial reporting standards in the EC, which has a common model of corporate reporting, and relatively common cultural perspective, leads one to be very conservative when predicting that global harmonization of reporting will be realized in the early twenty first century. Countries which have so much in common and such economic incentives to enhance the nature and content of corporate reporting, such as the EC nations, have experienced strong impediments to change; we will have to predict that countries with very diverse models of reporting, cultural backgrounds, and intercountry competitiveness will experience a tough road toward harmonization.

Data and Comparability Issues

The quality and availability of data is crucial to establishing accountability for performance. In the international environment, due to the absence of standardization of accounting rules, as well as the inherent risk in distanced operations, data integrity and reliability is often an almost insurmountable problem. Differences in measurement and recognition abound. Conversion of most international financial statements is necessary prior to analysis by investors, or prior to consolidation. Measurement pertains to timing, valuation, and recognition of transactions. Disclosure concerns the aggregation, labelling, and reporting of significant items.

For example, the Statement of Cash Flows mandated by SFAS #95 in the United States is not required in most countries of the world. Furthermore, cash flow is impossible to reconstruct from the existing disclosures of most other countries. Therefore, capital market participants will have to estimate the cash flow data by using surrogate information, and hope that their estimate is reasonably close to that actual, but unknown, cash flow. In situations such as this there are costs incurred in the location and analysis of data. Subsequent to that problem, the reliability of the analysis and surrogate factors present additional risk into the valuation model.

There is fairly wide diversity in reporting, even in the industrialized nations. For example, major IASC Standards set reporting and measurement standards in the following areas:

- consolidation policy

- inventory valuation

- statement of changes in financial position

- depreciation

- effects of changing price levels

- segmental reporting

- income tax reporting and allocation

- lease accounting

Diversity among relatively common backgrounds such as the United States, the UK, Canada, and the European Community is significant. Take depreciation as an example.[44] IAS No. 4 mandates disclosure of depreciation methods and expense for each major category of depreciable assets. The United States mandates aggregate disclosures. The UK requires major category disclosures. Canada mandates aggregate disclosures. The EC requires disclosure of changes during the year for each category of depreciable assets. In cases such as this one, if you are given only aggregate information on annual statements, there is no way for the analyst to generate the data by individual category. Thus, comparability and uniformity are impaired.

Other data issues, in addition to the quantity of information, pertain to the quality of information. Quality is often a function of other indices, such as regulatory environment, sophistication and number of professional accountants, cultural and historical considerations, and business complexity as seen in Figure 5.1.

Figure 5.1
Data Quality and Quantity Considerations in an International Setting

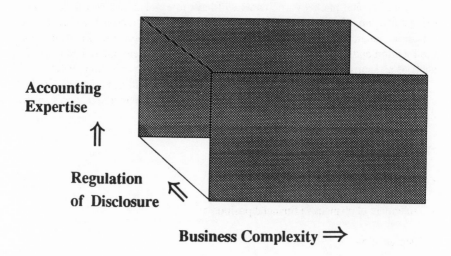

Accounting
Expertise

⇑

Regulation
of Disclosure ⬉

Business Complexity ⇒

If the regulatory environment both requires financial reporting in comparable formats, and requires audit of that information, the information may be deemed relatively reliable. But in situations where regulatory bodies such as the S.E.C. in the U.S. are either absent or sub-optimal in policing disclosures, annual reports may be less than forthcoming. With regard to the sophistication of the accounting profession in the environment of a particular country, it has been found that business sophistication typically precedes that of the accountants. This has led to an influx of non-national auditors in the many countries which have not yet been able to keep up with the demand for accounting services. (This dilemma is discussed below). The more scarce auditing resources are, the less comprehensive the individual audit will be, and there will be less penetration into the audit market as well. Business complexity means that the quality of the data may be compromised as it is aggregated and measurement problems may intrude on the reports. Multiple subsidiaries and a higher proportion of international subsidiaries make reports more complex and the quality of the data more suspect. This is particularly true if the regulatory environment is weak and there are not sufficient professional accountants to serve domestic industry.

The diversity of reporting rules, the complexity of multinational enterprises, and the sporadic application of regulation in many parts of the world mean that financial reports are difficult to evaluate. This situation, in turn, impinges on the ability to perform a meaningful and comprehensive performance audit. Without the development of standardized reporting categories, uniform data availability, and sufficient professional expertise, performance audits will be difficult to pursue. But performance management is just as critical in geographically diverse operations as it is in domestic ones. In fact, the diversity means that interpretation and utilization of traditional reports is even more difficult in the international domain. The value added by the performance audit under these circumstances is exponential.

The Development of Rapidly Emerging Economies

Perhaps the most challenging environment in which to assess and report on economy, efficiency, and effectiveness is in emerging nations. In them, professional personnel shortages to perform the audits combine with evolving regulatory agencies and reporting standards which may often be adopted on a voluntary basis. In economies where there is strong central government influence, the development and evolution of reporting and control mechanisms may happen rapidly.

This occurs because of two factors. First, there is usually historical precedent of mandated reports and codified standards. Second, uniformity of accounting and reporting is required for the central government to retain control of operations. In this environment, allocation of capital is made by the government, and public reporting of accountability and management effectiveness takes a secondary role in favor of government management of outputs.

The events of the 1990s in China and the Baltic countries, along with other previously Soviet-managed territories, mean that large economic forces are turning dramatically away from strong centrally managed productive power to financial status which requires participation and competition in capital markets. These changes impact broadly on capital users and capital providers in the emerging economies and mean that users of reports need reliable and timely information.

Furthermore, the new objective of linking inputs to outputs, as opposed to the previous focus on production, means that the development of performance information provides essential transition information in a market newly driven by users of financial and qualitative information.

In addition to the many areas of the world where national economies are moving from central control to full participation in capital markets and private enterprise, some nations are experiencing hyperinflation and the collapse of governmental ability to control debt and extranational flow of capital. In economies where this is the case special reporting needs are crucial. In the case of inflation, current accounting in most parts of the world does not include either holding period gains or monetary gains or losses. When significantly high inflation rates are experienced the absence of these adjustments make financial statements irrelevant. Managements and governments need to disclose more "soft" data and more qualitative data to show a relevant picture.

The Treadway Commission's Committee of Sponsoring Organizations (COSO) report is particularly useful to government and enterprises trying to cope with hyperinflation and national debt default. The report instructs firms to take a broad view of internal control and to issue more public reports on controls. For example, the expanded definition of internal control includes "ethical values, integrity, and competence," as well as "communication, managing change, and monitoring."[45]

In this enlightened viewpoint, the Committee asserts that internal control is "geared towards achieving an entity's objectives. Such objectives may pertain to the entity as a whole, such as maintaining a positive reputation."[46] Efficient and effective use of the entity's resources in achieving goals is particularly noted. Furthermore, the instruction to achieve effective communication between the firm and outside parties is included in the scope of assessment of internal control. Monitoring is broadened as a concept to include "reacting to input from auditors, regulators, and other parties." In this way, it may be expected that enhanced reporting from troubled economies may be achieved in the future.

Most international and national standards include review and reporting of internal control. If the expanded themes of internal control that are espoused by the COSO report infiltrate the international community, we may expect better information with which to appraise economy, efficiency, and effectiveness. The explicit recommendation of the COSO report, which includes managing change as a component of internal control, is of considerable value to emerging economies. Managing change includes being able to "identify, communicate, evaluate, and respond to change on a timely basis" and encompasses "economic, industry, regulatory, and operating environments."[47] The existence of comprehensive standards to enhance the reporting of nonfinancial data will make the reporting of performance more achievable. This is particularly relevant in emerging economies.

The Multinational Environment Poses Risks

There are significant risks for firms operating in a multinational environment, and performance audit which measures efficiency, effectiveness, and economy of the firm helps to manage those risks. Even companies which implemented TQM programs five years ago are finding, for example, that the quality control standards put forth by ISO 9000 regulations for international manufacturing quality are more stringent than their existing controls. The ISO 9000 standards mean that many companies are having to implement and formulate even more standards for performance and compliance controls. In this environment, quality assurance programs pay high yields. A manager at Taylor Forge Engineered Systems, Inc., which operates in Kansas and serves the oil, natural gas, and chemical industries by making tubing and piping, says, "Quality assurance under TQM relies more on planning for quality as opposed to inspecting for quality."[48] The concept of continuous quality advanced by TQM also needs to mean measurable outcomes, or performance reporting. Conference Board, in a comprehensive survey on continuous quality improvement, found that firms reported that while customer satisfaction is a valuable TQM boon, "results from this study suggest that those looking to TQM for a quick fix are likely to be disappointed."[49] With the ISO 9000 standards, customer satisfaction may be a necessary but not sufficient criterion for a competitive firm. Performance accountability will have to go much further. In a survey of large, diverse, multinational firms, about half of those polled responded that "improving productivity and efficiency is their number one management objective."[50] The next most common objective among these firms was that of managing growth.

In managing in the international environment, there are conceptually three prongs to an effort towards controlling risk.[51] One is policing, and that is the purview of the regulatory agencies. The second is auditing, which provides value by assurance that managers are operating in the interests of firm owners and other stakeholders. Increasingly, audit and auditors are seen as a form of insurance against financial losses due to the failure of a business. Audit firms, both domestic and international, are the deep pockets even when business failure rather than audit failure has occurred. The third prong is monitoring and that is achieved through accountability reporting.

Only accountability reporting manages risk by providing information to stakeholders with competing utility functions. For example, in a multinational firm, several countries compete for income taxes generated by firm profits. Disposal of toxic waste must be achieved, but is least cost (dumping in a developing nation) the overriding criterion, or should the waste be transported to a nation who has the technology in place to diffuse the toxicity? In most cases, really, competition between stakeholders is not readily solved by international law. In fact, "regulatory failure," i.e., the result when the repercussions of regulatory laws are more detrimental than the economic inefficiencies which the laws attempt to cure, is not uncommon. The phenomenon is particularly intense because complexity in capital markets generates complexity in regulation. Then, the ability of nations to integrate effectively is impaired.

Particular risk areas which respond to economy, efficiency, and effectiveness reporting are:

- Communication systems

- Environmental variables

- Cultural differences

- Accounting measurement rules

- Accounting disclosure rules

- Availability of audit services

- Language, terminology, and technical reporting

- Differences in business organization and entity types

- Operations, including manufacturing, banking, and equity markets

- Foreign currency translation policies

- Comparability of data between firms

- Comparability of data between nations

In managing international risk, financial reporting is not sufficient for capital market participants, even when supplemented by TQM. Rather, reporting how management has coped with opportunities and challenges regarding the above factors provides a more complete and usable mechanism for evaluation of performance.

Lack of Comparability in Accounting Reports and Effects on Performance Evaluation

Specific differences among nations on accounting policies will impact upon the performance measurement system used to evaluate economy, efficiency, and effectiveness. Standardization of accounting rules make the uniform reporting of performance more quickly and easily achieved. A listing of common differences is shown in Figure 5.2.

However, internal control and performance reporting are possible even without standardization. Management planning and control systems are often affected by cultural differences, and research has demonstrated that these differences are often significant.[52] Particularly troubling is that fact that users' needs are different between nations. Add to this the negative cost/benefit relationship in nations where the quality of data is compromised and performance reports in some applications may provide only generalistic impressions of oversight by management. Nevertheless, there is a positive effect in having management define specific goals and measure both tendency and dispersion in the achievement of goals. Explicit reporting on such straightforward trends such as asset productivity, growth and product diversification, strategic planning, and quality control is beneficial and obtainable in almost any business entity. The difficulty often arises from shortages of expertise in performance auditing and lack of comparability in the reporting mechanism.

Figure 5.2
Major Diversity Factors in Multinational Reporting

Reporting Policy

a) Marketable Securities	■ Lower of Cost or Market
b) Cost Basis	■ Historical or Price Level Adjusted
c) Consolidation	■ Full or Partial
d) Goodwill	■ Amortized or Unamortized
e) Research & Development	■ Expense or Capitalized
f) Pension Funds	■ Balance Sheet Inclusion or Balance Sheet Exclusion
g) Foreign Currency	■ Temporal Method or Other

MANAGING GLOBAL AUDIT OPERATIONS FOR ACCOUNTABILITY

Auditing Domination by Big Firms May Foster Performance Audit

As has been discussed, both financial audit and performance audit are thwarted to some extent by insufficient professional expertise in emerging nations to conduct such investigations. The concept of emerging nations is used here to depict both lesser developed nations which are becoming industrialized, as well as industrialized nations which are abandoning centralized economies in favor of capitalistic forms of enterprise and competition for capital.

There is some research evidence that major international accounting firms are dominating the market for audit services in newly emerging economies.[53] This may, in fact, foster performance audit. These large international firms have both the resources and the expertise to engage in comprehensive auditing, and are certain to recognize economies of scale in investigating the operations of large multinational firms.

Furthermore, the existence of firm-specific audit guidelines as well as firm audit procedures acts as somewhat of a standardization mechanism in the absence of other national and professional guidelines. The tendency of large firms to dominate in audits of multinational firms reduces risk and cost.[54] While many trade barriers exist between nations, it appears at present that the barriers to entry in auditing services are minimal. The primary inhibiting factor pertains to the increased risk of auditing due to diversity and data quality issues in an international setting. In some cases this risk may be managed by using local or affiliated firms where the start-up cost for larger firms is too great.

A PERFORMANCE AUDIT MODEL FOR MULTINATIONAL OPERATIONS OF PRIVATE SECTOR FIRMS

In this section, the practice of performance auditing is adapted for the multinational firm. The adaptation of the model includes considerations of additional risk factors, as well as considerations of aggregation and reporting of information. Program, product, and strategic reviews are possible across national boundaries, and reports summarizing the results of operations with regard to economy, efficiency, and effectiveness are achieved through the utilization of performance audit. The audit's review function adds credibility to the reports of management, and thus enhances capital market efficiency and ultimately reduces the cost of capital to private firms.

In the United States, Statement of Auditing Standards No. 8 addresses the auditor's responsibility for reviewing information which is other than financial information. This auditing standard includes information relating to performance evaluation which is included along with other audited statements. The Statement does not require auditors to independently verify such data, and no formalized standards exist for private sector performance reporting at this time. In the public sector there are formal guidelines for performance reporting, particularly under the Chief Financial Officers Act. OMB Bulletin No. 91-15 addresses the need to include a flexible format so that information "useful to senior managers, program managers, and financial mangers in making decisions" may be included.[55] Practices and procedures for mandated performance audits of federal entities is included in the Yellow Book, *Standards for Audit of Governmental Organizations, Programs, Activities and Functions.* The General Accounting Office oversees the generation of rules of practice for performance auditors in this sector.

The absence of such promulgated standards in the private sector, combined with the inherent riskiness of the multinational marketplace, makes the development of a comprehensive, consistent, and ultimately codified private sector model compelling. One useful model in the public sector assesses data by appropriateness, relevance, accessibility, economy, and impact.[56] This model may be adapted successfully into evaluating the scope and content of the performance audit. As has been mentioned, most multinational organizations are familiar with some form of quality review or quality audit. In implementing performance audit, the added rigor of the audit process and knowledge of the audit target factors of economy, efficiency, and effectiveness drive the process to be useful to a wide range of stakeholders. In Brand-Rex Co., one manager noted, "You're looking at our operation eight hours a day, five days a week; but the team performing the audit are outsiders and they see things you can't . . . Their feedback is always helpful."[57] A private sector perspective in the international area must focus on a wide range of products, services, and markets. One company uses a "balanced scorecard" approach which specifies objectives and measures for financial goals, customer relations, business development, and technology and innovation.[58]

While the general model of performance auditing specified earlier is applicable to private multinational firms, some adaptations are useful. The amplified model follows, which addresses the unique characteristics of performance auditing in an international setting.

Developing Accountability Relationships

The mandate for performance reporting may be from one or several sources in a multinational private corporation setting. The main possibilities are: contract authority, corporate authority, and government authority. In addition, there may be multiple or overlapping responsibilities as shown in Figure 5.3.

Contract

Contract authority may be initiated by the local entity, by the regional division of the firm, or by the directors of the consolidated entity. In the contract, the scope, nature, and reporting authority should be designated in a letter to the auditors.

Multinational complexity is introduced because of the absence of coherent reporting standards and the intricacies of diverse international accounting and other data. However, perhaps the most important factor in a contract audit is the specification of the performance standards and outcomes which inevitably evolve from the process of accountability reporting.

Corporate

A regional, divisional, or consolidated entity authority in a private multinational firm may undertake to have one or more of the international operations of a private

Figure 5.3
Developing Accountability Relationships in a Multinational Setting

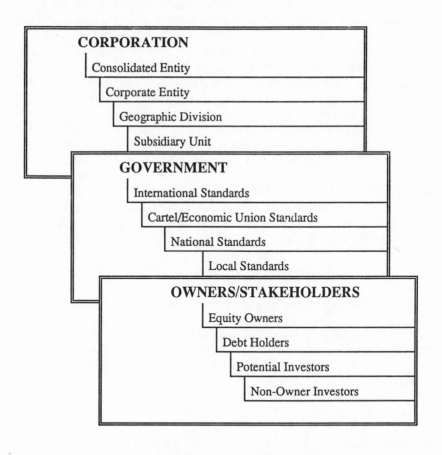

firm evaluated for economy, efficiency, or effectiveness. In this type of case, the interrelationships between the audit target and other operations of the firm usually need to be integrated in some fashion. This is because data availability, standard-setting, capital allocations, and profit targets may not be under the control of the local entity. In the corporate situation there will be synergistic benefits from auditing several similar components of the entire organization, rather than initiating a piecemeal approach by targeting a few distantly located operations.

Figure 5.4
Reporting Targets in a Multinational Environment

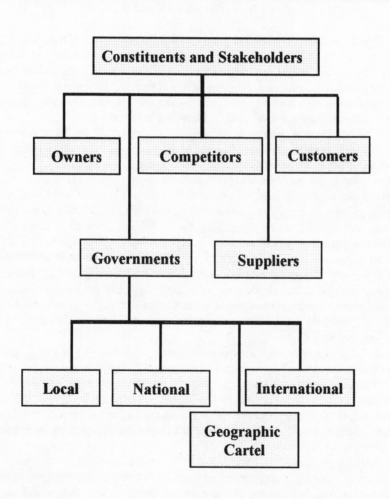

Government

A government mandate may stem from a legislative statute or from a standard-setting body, such as the IASC or the United Nations. For example, in some situations, the World Bank has required accountability reporting prior to releasing funds for capital projects in many parts of the world. At the present time, the formally promulgated standards which exist for performance auditing pertain exclusively to the public sector. However, as this type of audit expands more and more into the private sector, the development of private sector standards is sure to follow.

Reporting Congruence for Performance Evaluation

Trying to define the different groups of stakeholders in a multinational firm is difficult and fraught with unknowns. In a model of constituents and stakeholders in an international circumstance, consider factions of owners, creditors, and customers at the firm level; government and suppliers at the level of operations; and local, national, geographic cartel or economic union members; plus laws and regulatory units at the international level. This is illustrated in Figure 5.4.

This is, of course, parallel to defining and categorizing constituent groups for accountability reporting purposes. In many of the groups goals for accountability will overlap. In others, reporting goals may be rather specific, or mandated by law. In still others, local union laws or banking requirements may be used to configure reporting content and style. Consider, for example, the complexity found by Manufacturers Hanover Corporation in trying to set up an integrated audit for operations in the United States and the UK. The organization found different systems of management information which impeded integrated audit possibilities.[59] In addition, the Catholic Relief Services has initiated a program to audit operations in over twenty countries each year even though the individual environments lack comparability.[60] Particular national differences include the presence of the Foreign Corrupt Practices Act in the United States which has no comparable law in any other part of the world, and the fact that highly standardized expectations for internal control exist in the United States, but not in many other nations.

In Brazil, for example, corporate entity form is more likely to be a joint venture, consortium, or partnership rather than a corporation.[61] The general consistency with international accounting standards, and the existence of a positive regulatory environment for financial disclosures has fostered international investment in Brazil. Even so, these reporting requirements are not necessarily consistent with practices in other nations, and while they produce a positive reporting environment, international complexity persists.

In some environments, for example, there have been initiatives to change the traditional reporting of components on financial statements. For example, in some Islamic nations, the reporting of interest is discouraged. In a study of differences between Japanese and U.S. firms, for example, it was found that culture did, indeed, affect the overall nature and content of reporting.[62] The liberalization of international investment in mainland China has created many joint venture operations with other nations. Because the audit profession in China cannot absorb the demand transfer of technology in audit services is being experienced,[63] as large multinational audit firms enter and bring with them their own cultural background in producing performance and accountability studies. In the emerging capitalist economy in Croatia, an Act on Accountancy has been passed which adopts the model of the EC and makes Croatian business accountable for fulfilling IASC standards.[64] Advances in standardization of data accumulation and reporting will enhance the quality and quantity of performance audits accomplished. Congruity of multinational reports follows congruence of general standards of public disclosures as seen in Figure 5.5.

The pyramiding of differences in a multinational firm adds complexity to the reporting process. But increasing practice and standardization in international markets will ultimately mean that accountability reporting will be more universally available and more comprehensible to diverse groups of stakeholders.

Standards of Measurement and Evidence in a Multinational Setting

The complexity and diversity introduced by a multinational environment means that a performance audit is likely to absorb more resources and be subject to additional risk over audit in a single-nation situation. Some elements which need to be addressed include knowledge of the entity, audit objectives, scope, criteria for inclusion in the audit and the audit report, qualification of audit evidence, and timeliness of the report. Entity knowledge will be more complex because the performance auditors will need to become familiar not only with the parent organization, but also the local environment in which the audited entity operates and the risks that pertain to that specific arena. Furthermore, in attempting to obtain knowledge of the entity, comparability studies are likely to be more complex than those in a single nation. The auditor will need to obtain an understanding of similar organizations in the local area, the geographic region or cartel, and geographically diverse operations of the consolidated firm.

Scope considerations will depend upon many more factors, and perhaps a more complex understanding of factors, than in the domestic-only firm. For example, variability of staff and professionals to conduct the audit will be a factor in scope. Increased costs due to geographic diversity may also limit or become a factor in the scope of the audit. In addition, the firm will have to determine the frequency of the performance evaluation and reporting. Is this a one-time contract, with limited distribution of results and little ongoing monitoring, or is the audit to be conducted on a regular basis and given broad public distribution to owners, creditors, and other stakeholders? Another factor in the designation of scope will be the time period covered. For joint ventures, development stage enterprises, and similar situations, the time period may cover the entire life of the entity; in other circumstances an annual time period, or a three-year cycle of audit investigation may be appropriate. Finally, decisions about comprehensiveness will necessarily be made. The audit scope may

Figure 5.5
International Reporting Diversity

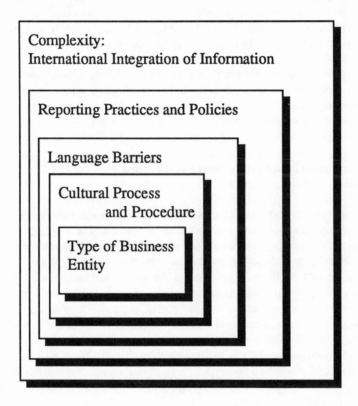

specify the entire operation, a portion of the operation, one line of goods or services, or a particular division or branch. Again, integration of the performance audit among entity units is synergistic. Results will be enhanced by having one product line targeted across all entity operations and integrating the reports rather than having a limited focus on the entire operation of one entity. This is because multidisciplinary teams must be set up for an effective performance audit and the economies of scale emerge from the team usage.

Audit evidence is problematic in an international setting because there is no GAAP from which to base the underlying reliance on internal control for private firms and for multinational firms. Furthermore, the quality, availability, and sustainability of the information system used to obtain performance evidence may vary widely among units of a multinational enterprise. Criteria for including data elements in the performance of an accountability study or performance audit in a multinational firm include many factors.[65] This is illustrated in Figure 5.6.

In order to qualify data in the analysis, the traditional components of data quality are used. These criteria are supplemented then by the need for country-by-country comparability between local, national, multinational, and international operations.

In the worldwide operations of private firms, there are three types of riskiness of data, and these types are compounded by the diversity and complexity of global operations. The three types of risk are: inherent risk, control risk, and detection risk. Figure 5.7 illustrates this.

Inherent risk pertains to the fact that in all data measurement and data specification there is intrinsic variability and tendency toward some specification error. Inherent risk in a performance audit context means that there is indeed a real and present risk that value-for-money considerations were not attained. That is, there is inherent risk that economy, efficiency, and effectiveness of operations are not uniformly present.

Control risk is a term applied to the existence and operation of policies and procedures to control operations in achieving value-for-money. In a traditional audit, internal control is the first level of reliance for the decisions regarding audit scope and process. In the performance audit position, controls which are relevant are those pertaining to ensuring that economy, efficiency, and effectiveness are achieved. To the extent that language, culture, and reporting differences exist among nations, control risk is compounded for private multinational firms.

Detection risk pertains to audit risk. That is, in the audit process there is a possibility that the auditor will not find evidence of performance deviation, when, in fact there is deviation; alternatively, there is the possibility that the auditor will find or detect failure to perform with due regard for economy, efficiency, and effectiveness, when there is no deviation in the organization. The defined risk here, then, is one of mismeasuring, either positively or negatively, the actual state of affairs. The most troubling risk to private audit firms in the audit process is failure to detect employee malfeasance, management fraud, asset misuse, and obfuscation of failure to achieve targeted goals. These problems are endemic in some cultures and extremely rare in others. Thus, the presence of international cultural differences is clearly going to play a role in the detection risk of the performance audit team.

Standards of Field Work and Reporting in a Multinational Setting

Field work in performance auditing includes planning, scheduling, costing-out, supervising, and performing the audit. Reporting includes adhering to schedule, determining the content and form of disclosures, and defining a distribution list. In the sphere of international performance reporting, both internal and external factors will

Figure 5.6
Criteria for Data in Multinational Reporting

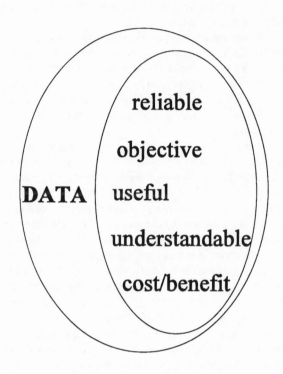

contribute to risk and complexity. Both internal and external dimensions affect field work and reporting for multinationals. The performance audit will encompass a wider range of external factors and also a much broader range in internal factors. The multinational firm will be able to exert minimal control over the external factors, but may exert moderate control over most of the internal dimensions as shown in Figure 5.8.

The external considerations are significant and include barriers to trade, regulatory restrictions, social and human resource habits, political stability and governmental control mechanisms, and macroeconomic components of business decision making. Internal considerations are comprised of elements such as business policies, business systems, employment and management practices, codes of conduct for the firm, and centralization tendencies of the entity. These components will have to be assessed in the local environment of the audit target and reassessed during the field work. They will impact on the ability of the auditors to execute the performance evaluation and

Figure 5.7
Evidence and Data Risks Multiply in an International Context

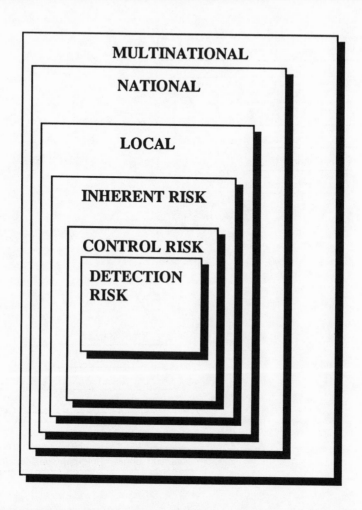

MULTINATIONAL

NATIONAL

LOCAL

INHERENT RISK

CONTROL RISK

DETECTION RISK

accomplish the accountable reporting goals as defined by the engagement. While these components also operate to an extent in single-nation firms, they are compounded in quantity and degree in a multinational setting. The combinations and permutations of effects make predictions precarious, and sustainability of the audit results are questionable in the event of significant uncertainties. Therefore, the background review of these factors will alert the readers of performance reports about the risk factors and degree of variability of the findings.

The point has been made for the public sector that budget deficits and decreasing

Figure 5.8
Field Work Control in the Absence of International Performance Audit Standards

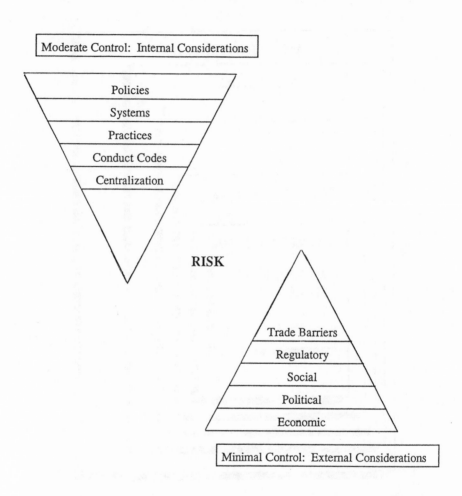

rates of tax increases have meant that more performance must be achieved with fewer resources. However, it is ironic that cost-cutting often includes reducing funds budgeted for audits which measure and report on economy, efficiency, and effectiveness of operations.[66] It is just under these circumstances, in the private sector as well, where profit margins are being squeezed and competition comes from more and more external markets, that performance audit will realize its maximum utility and achieve its finest cost/benefit relationship.

NOTES

1. Brian Boland. "Performance Auditing Techniques and Reporting." *Australian Accountant* (May 1987): 57–60.

2. Richard C. Tracy. "Performance Auditing Techniques and Reporting." *Australian Accountant* (May 1987): 57–60.

3. Keiichi Tsuji. "New Trends in Government Audit in Japan." *International Journal of Government Auditing* (July 1988): 8–16.

4. Richard P. Kusserow. "Program Inspections." *The Government Accountants Journal* (Spring 1984): 1–6.

5. M. Hendricks. "Service Delivery Assessment: Qualitative Evaluations at the Cabinet Level." *New Directions for Program Evaluation: Federal Efforts to Develop New Evaluation Methods*. N. Smith, ed. San Francisco: Jossey-Bass. 1981.

6. Kusserow. 1984.

7. John J. Glynn. *Value for Money Auditing in the Public Sector. Research Studies in Accounting*. London: Prentice Hall International. 1985. p. 133.

8. For applications of the internal control review and governmental performance audit, see the following: James P. Wesberry. "Opportunities to Help Improve Government Financial Management in Latin America." *The Government Accountants Journal* (Summer 1981): 36–45; and, by the U.S. Comptroller General. *Training and Related Efforts Needed to Improve Financial Management in the Third World*. Washington, DC: U.S.G.P.O. 1979.

9. Boland. 1987.

10. A discussion on the different definitions and applications of performance audit is contained in Lee Parker. "Towards Value for Money Audit Policy." *Australian Accountant* (December 1986): 79–82.

11. *Comprehensive Auditing in Canada: The Provincial Legislative Audit Perspective*. Ottawa: Canadian Comprehensive Auditing Foundation. 1985

12. *Value for Money in Municipalities: A Practitioner's Guide*. Ottawa: Canadian Comprehensive Auditing Foundation. 1984.

13. For the audit standards, see "Value for Money Audits." *Accountancy* (November 1987): 142–44.

14. See Lee Parker. 1986.

15. Parker. 1986.

16. Glynn. 1985.

17. Tsuji. 1988.

18. Tsuji. 1988.

19. Neil Adams. "Definitions, Objectives and Limitations of Performance Auditing—An AAO Perspective." *Australian Accountant* (August 1987): 29–31.

20. John Hegarty. "GATT: A Chance to Take the Lead." *Accountancy* 113:1206 (February 1994): 72–73.

21. Wen Shuo and Stephen C. Yam. "Audit Profile: People's Republic of China." International Journal of Government Auditing (October 1987): 1–12.

22. G. Peter Wilson. "Expanded Cooperation Between Internal and External Audit in Government." *International Journal of Government Auditing* (January 1988): 9–10, 19.

23. Emma Hippolyte. "The Canada-St. Lucia Comprehensive Project." *International Journal of Government Auditing* (January 1987): 12–24.

24. Muhammad Aram Khan. "Implementing Performance Auditing in Pakistan." *International Journal of Government Auditing* (October 1986): 15–17.

25. Michael L. Jadjiloizou. "Audit of Capital Projects." *International Journal of Government Auditing* (July 1988): 13–15.

26. "Methodologies and Practices in the Audit of Public Debt: Focus on Malaysia, the Philippines, and Thailand." *International Journal of Government Auditing* (October 1988): 8–17.

27. "Methodologies and Practices." 1988.

28. "Methodologies and Practices." 1988.

29. Tsuji. 1988.

30. D. A. Dewar. "The Auditor General and the Examination of Policy." *International Journal of Government Auditing* (April 1986): 14–16.

31. Shuo and Yam. 1987.

32. Anthony D. Clyne. "Efficiency Audits, Australian Style." *The Government Accountants Journal* (Spring 1986): 60–61.

33. Hippolyte. 1987.

34. R. Douglas Thomas. "International Accounting Standards." *Chartered Accountant Magazine* (October 1977): 49–50.

35. Alister K. Mason. "The Evolution of International Accounting Standards." In *Multinational Accounting: A Research Framework for the Eighties*. Frederick Choi, ed. Ann Arbor, MI: UMI Research Press. 1981. pp. 155–70.

36. Mason. 1981. p. 161.

37. Lane A. Daley and Gerhard G. Mueller. "Accounting in the Arena of World Politics: Crosscurrents of International Standard-Setting Activities." *Global Accounting Perspectives*. Jagdish Sheth and Abdolreza Eshghi, eds. Cincinnati: Southwestern Publishing Co. 1989. pp. 21–32.

38. Daley and Mueller. 1989. p. 37.

39. Robert K. Elliott. "The Future of Audits: The Power of Information Technology is Threatening the Audit Function." *Journal of Accountancy* (September 1994): 74–82.

40. Elliott. 1994. p. 76.

41. S. J. Gray. "The Impact of International Accounting Differences from a Security-Analysis Perspective: Some European Evidence." *Journal of Accounting Research* 18:1 (Spring 1980): 64–76; also, W. G. Frank. "An Empirical Analysis of International Accounting Principles." *Journal of Accounting Research* 17:1 (Autumn 1979): 369–605.

42. Adolph Enthoven. "International Management Accounting: Its Scope and Standards." *The International Journal of Accounting, Education, and Research* 17:2 (Spring 1982): 59–74. Also, Frederick Choi, et al. "Analyzing Foreign Financial Statements: The Use of Misuse of International Ratio Analysis." *Journal of International Business Studies* 14:1 (Spring/Summer 1983): 113–32.

43. Gerhard G. Mueller, Helen Gernon, and Gary K. Meeks. *Accounting, An International Perspective*. Third Edition. Burr Ridge, IL: Irwin. 1994. p. 45.

44. Ernst and Whinney. *International Accounting Standards* (September 1982): 64–71.

45. Treadway Commission. "An Integrated Framework for Internal Control." March 12, 1991.

46. Treadway Commission. 1991.

47. Treadway Commission. 1991.

48. Grant Thornton International. "Changing a Quality Program to Meet ISO 9000." *Manufacturing Issues* 4:3 (Summer 1993): 6.

49. The Conference Board. *Report Number 974: Employee Buy-in to Total Quality*. New York: The Conference Board. 1991. p. 39.

50. BDO Seidman. *Pulse of the Middle Market*. New York: BDO Seidman/BDO Binder International. 1991. p. 17.

51. Anthony Steele. *Audit Risk and Audit Evidence: The Bayesian Approach to Statistical Auditing*. London: Academic Press Limited. 1992. p. 54.

52. L. J. Daley, G. L . Sundem, and Y. Kondo. "Attitudes Toward Financial Control Systems in the U.S. and Japan." *Journal of International Business Studies* 16:2 (Fall 1985): 91–110.

53. John W. Eichenseher. "The Effects of Foreign Operations on Domestic Auditor Selection." *Journal of Accounting, Auditing, and Finance* 8:3 (Spring 1985): 195–209.

54. Manuel Tipgos. "Potential Liabilities in International Accounting Practice." *Journal of Accounting Research* (Spring 1980): 161–90.

55. Alexis Stowe. "Auditing Performance Measurement Reporting." *Government Accountants Journal* (Winter 1992): 23–36.

56. Narayan Persaud and David R. DiSlvo. "Some Things About Surveys They forgot to Teach Us in Social Science 301: The Performance Audit Perspective." *Government Accountants Journal* (Winter 1992): 37–48.

57. Grant Thornton International. "Meeting ISO 9000 Quality Standards Helps Brand-Rex Compete." *Manufacturing Issues* 3:1 (Winter 1992): 8.

58. Robert S. Kaplan and David P. Norton. "The Balanced Scorecard—Measures that Drive Performance." *Harvard Business Review* (January/February 1992): 71–79.

59. Gerald Vinton. "International Audit in Perspective: a U.S./ U.K. Comparison." *Internal Auditing* 6:4 (Spring 1991): 3–9.

60. Vinton. 1991.

61. Brazil: Foreign Investment." *Euromoney* (April 1994): 14–17.

62. Robert Bloom, Susan Long, and Marilynn Collins. "Japanese and American Accounting: Explaining the Differences." *Advances in International Accounting* 6 (1994): 265–84.

63. Paul Sweeney. "Accounting: Making Sense of Chinese Books." *Global Finance* 7:4 (April 1993): 29–30.

64. Vladimir Filipovic. "Croatia: Accounting and Audit Laws." *East European Business Law* 93 (May 1993): 25.

65. Public Sector Accounting and Auditing Committee of the Canadian Institute of Chartered Accountants. *Public Sector Auditing Guideline 1: Planning Value-for-Money Audits*. Ottawa, Canada: Canadian Institute of Chartered Accountants. 1990. p. 11.

66. Linda J. Blessing. "New Opportunities: A CPA's Primer on Performance Auditing." *Journal of Accountancy* (May 1991): 58–68.

Chapter 6

The Future of Performance Auditing: Problems and Unresolved Issues

INTRODUCTION

Value-for-money auditing is being implemented throughout the world; it is primarily used in the public sector where performance measures are difficult to specify, but the private sector is finding that it is useful in a profit-oriented environment as well. Currently, the absence of consistent generally accepted accounting and auditing principles for performance auditing has hindered the adoption of the technique. However, implementation guidelines and public sector reporting requirements are now sufficiently sophisticated for new users to easily adapt the process to their own organizations.

In this chapter the future of performance auditing is addressed by examining current unresolved issues and practice problems. First, the notion that comprehensive auditing requires adoption of comprehensive accounting is addressed. Next, the needed integration of managerial and financial accounting for the purpose of making decision making more systematic, and accountability more transparent, is explored. This discussion is followed by an examination of the effect of a trend in developed nations. The move away from capital assets toward human assets and knowledge workers means that very different audit evidence must be obtained. Then, related to the trend toward human assets, but standing alone as a separate issue, is the concern with civil liberties of managers, and the economic and legal effects of widespread disclosure of performance audit results. The penultimate section addresses the strategies of *resourcing* and *referencing* which apply uniquely to the practice of performance auditing. The final issue investigated concerns the political dimension of performance reporting and societal allocation issues involved in escalating the number and depth of social accounting disclosures.

COMPREHENSIVE ACCOUNTING FOR COMPREHENSIVE AUDITING

Current financial accounting standards have severe shortcomings when evaluated for purposes of comprehensive auditing. For example, one of the major assets in the public sector is the human resource base; this is not recorded under traditional financial accounting. Another example relates to the very nature of fund accounting in the public sector; while each fund statement is useful in assessing the financial status of that element, cumulating fund statements into the comprehensive financial report is not easily accomplished without losing critical detail. A further problem is that there is no motive to save money in the public sector. As long as a manager conforms to budget objectives, he appears to be efficient. Traditional flexible budgeting systems do not encourage managers to set tighter standards for themselves, but rather motivate managers to accept given standards and live within them. Public sector budgeting, used as a control mechanism, may stifle creativity and, in extreme circumstances where there is dysfunctional timing, encourage unnecessary spending because carryovers are not permitted into a new budget period.

Yet another drawback of traditional financial reporting is that replacement cost accounting, or at a minimum price level adjusted accounting, is rarely used now that it is no longer required to be reported. This inflation factor, when ignored, understates the true cost of providing goods and services, and therefore overstates productivity. Finally, all too often in both the public and the private sectors, outputs of goods and services are measured in units produced or distributed, or dollars expended. The units produced measurement fails miserably to alert management to reasons output goals were not achieved, or where opportunities for cost savings exist at a particular output level. Managerial accountants often refer to this unfortunate information block phenomenon as "too little, too late."

Similarly, the output of goods and services is measured in historical terms, rather than proactive financial accounting. Once money is expended, it is, by definition, no longer under the control of management. Therefore, proactive systems of management information must be used so that management makes optimal decisions; furthermore, top management cannot wait until the financial reports are prepared to evaluate performance. By then they are no longer in control of the situation, and can only correct in the future. Rather, management needs "real time" systems. These enable both operational decision-making managers, as well as strategic top management performance evaluators, to adjust operations in the present, as well as correct for the future.

The point is, the quantity, the quality, and the timing of accounting information must be more comprehensive in order to take full advantage of performance auditing. Both accounting systems, as well as qualitative information, need more depth. In addition, control systems need to encompass more than safeguarding assets and controlling expenses. More economic considerations such as opportunity costs and capital maintenance reflections should also be included. Risk analysis of business decisions and sensitivity analysis of the underlying economic assumptions should be built into the control systems. The pervasiveness of the information systems, and the comprehensiveness of the data collected will provide the optimum conditions for effective performance audit.

INTEGRATION OF MANAGERIAL AND FINANCIAL ACCOUNTING

Managerial accounting and financial accounting are both used in the performance audit evaluation. This is because the performance audit includes consideration of the financial position of the firm: its compliance with applicable laws and regulations, its control of operations, and its managerial effectiveness. In this context, both the quantitative data from the accounting system, as well as the less easily modeled decision making of management is evaluated. For example, if, in the financial system, money has been diverted to inappropriate purposes, such as bribes which violate the Foreign Corrupt Practices Act, or no-interest loans to officers or directors, audit evidence and current audit procedures are available to discover and report on the malfeasance.

But consider, for a moment, the senior executive who has a proven history of being an effective decision maker. This executive may well use a heuristic, experiential, shoot-from-the-hip approach to decision making. Since we cannot model his decision making, and cannot therefore trace the information he uses, or the weighting of the information components, or the thought process, we cannot audit these elements with more traditional techniques. Rather, the auditor may have to rely on peer review information on this manager's decision making, or on other outside expert opinion regarding his effectiveness in making decisions. In addition, output measures alone will not be the key, even if they are qualitative, because he may be a long-term rather than short-term maximizer.

This, then, is the complexity of the performance audit; the audit procedures used to obtain audit evidence vary from confirming receivables to asking other managers what they think about the manager in question. The managerial accounting system, which uses economic concepts and probabilistic quantification, needs to be merged with the financial accounting system, which uses GAAP-based numbers and single value reporting.

Data Migration

This migration of managerial accounting into financial accounting is already beginning to occur. For example, consider the actuarial valuation and current value accounting used in the reporting of pensions on financial statements. Furthermore, the current turf ambiguity between the Financial Accounting Standards Board and the Governmental Accounting Standards Board is reflective of the need to have a broader base of accounting alternatives available to business versus nonbusiness entities, as well as different and specialized accounting procedures within the industry sectors. The migration of managerial accounting into financial accounting is also symptomatic of the widely expanded reporting being done within the context of "Management Discussion and Analysis" reports appended to traditional annual reports. Many managers simply feel that the financial reports do not reflect fully the results of operations, and have seized an opportunity to prepare and disseminate more relevant information to shareholders.

Because the performance auditor must carefully evaluate both the traditional financial accounting data, in addition to proprietary managerial accounting information, the trend toward merging the two systems fosters performance auditing. Performance auditing, in turn, fosters better accountability. Furthermore, consistent and professionally adopted generally accepted accounting principles and generally accepted auditing standards for performance auditing would be expected to increase the willingness of auditors, particularly in the private sector, to participate fully in performance auditing and to render opinions on performance audit statements.

Regulatory Failure

As an example, take the savings and loan institutions in crisis in the United States. It has taken billions of public dollars to bail out the financial institutions, which are privately held, and many of which were systematically bled of their profits by inept managers. Some of the savings and loans were victims of macroeconomic events, including eroded oil prices, which in turn choked off regional growth in some areas. But many other institutions were victims of poor management, including undercollateralized loans, a high proportion of high-risk loans, and poor loan documentation. Further problems were diversification into business segments in which the bank had no prior experience, unreasonable management compensation and perquisites, managerial confusion between personal and business expenses, and consistent underaccrual of reserves for loan losses.

On the other hand, financial institutions in the United States are among the most highly regulated of any industry. The high degree of regulation includes pervasively mandated financial reporting to the public and federal oversight agencies. One may reasonably whine, "If all of this financial reporting does not alert regulators and the public of impending disaster, what more can be done?" And one familiar with value-for-money auditing may equally respond, "It is not how *much* is being reported, the problem is *what* is being reported." For, in the final analysis, while the numbers should have told the story, the real reason for the collapse was not the obvious one of illiquidity, but rather, problems in *management control*. In short, there were accountability problems which went undiagnosed until it was too late.

Performance auditing, through utilization of a systematic, comprehensive, and integrated evaluation of management decision making and strategic planning, would have been useful here as an independent review of systems. Furthermore, if reporting of performance audit results had taken place and sunshine laws for performance audit results were within Generally Accepted Auditing Standards (GAAS), managements of savings and loans would have had a powerful incentive to keep a clean house. In order for the public and regulators to be proactive in the savings and loan crisis they needed both managerial and financial information. Performance auditing provides the needed integration and improves accountability reporting.

INTEGRATION OF HUMAN RESOURCE ACCOUNTING INTO FINANCIAL STATEMENTS

Performance auditing has been particularly useful in the public sector because it provides for human resources to be evaluated systematically and to be held accountable for their management. While cost systems have traditionally evaluated productivity of labor, knowledge workers— i.e., those who jobs are nonrepetitive and require judgments based on nonrepetitive inputs—have been difficult to track. Productivity measures for management and other knowledge workers are elusive. Under performance auditing knowledge workers are evaluated by looking at qualitative output measures; furthermore, the evaluation is done by an independent audit team and looks at the management system as a comprehensive unit rather than just the sum of individual outputs of individual managers.

Human resource accounting is not widely utilized at present. Performance audit professionals have an opportunity to expand the traditional reporting system to include human assets which are currently unbooked. This will provide better accounting systems as well as better accountability of human resources.

CIVIL LIBERTIES AND PERFORMANCE AUDIT DISCLOSURES

Performance auditing discloses more information, in more depth, and with greater clarity in reporting in most cases than is currently available to the public. This is true whether the performance audit is done in the public or the private sector. Due to the absence of Generally Accepted Governmental Auditing Standards (GAGAS) or GAAS in many nations for private sector applications, there is a minefield in front of auditors and corporations who want to disclose performance audit results. Even in the public sector, local, state (provincial), and federal managers may ask why it is appropriate that their performance evaluation be done in public, rather than privately. When a public sector institution is poorly managed it reflects badly on all managers, even if some are exemplary. Take, for example, the U.S. Housing and Urban Development brouhaha over incredibly lax internal controls for sales, loans, and management of public housing projects. The reputation of the entire organization was tarnished and many managers may have felt that they were convicted without a trial.

Charles Bowsher, as a Comptroller General of the United States, expressed concern over the omnipresent, but sometimes shallow, reporting of performance audit results by the media. He estimated that 80 percent of the public hearings concerning federal audits have extensive television coverage. The General Accounting Office performs numerous and extended performance audits which they often designate as "program reviews." To be useful the reports have to be easily readable and must contain executive summaries; the media often glosses over all of the reporting of the systems which are in control and tends to consider newsworthy only the management horror stories of systems entirely out of control. The public needs access to, and assurance, that the majority of the significant management functions are, in fact, being performed adequately.

Currently, reporting negatively about management performance may encourage shareholder lawsuits against corporations revealing performance audit results. Furthermore, management will want to have an opportunity to respond to the performance audit report to make sure that it is evenhanded and not political. Many nations in which performance auditing is currently practiced require management to respond to the performance audit report, whether or not it is made public; this enhances the commitment to accountability. However, the issue of private sector privacy over performance audit reports will have to be resolved at the level of financial reporting standard-setting bodies.

RESOURCING AND REFERENCING: AUDITING THE AUDITORS

Sanford Osler, with Ontario Hydro in Canada, and John Simonette of the U.S. General Accounting Office, suggest two new concepts which may well become commonly used in the future jargon of performance auditing. *Resourcing* refers to the staffing strategy of the performance audit. *Referencing* refers to the thematic content of the performance audit report. Both concepts provide insight into control of the performance audit itself.

Resourcing

The term *resourcing* highlights the tremendous diversity of work experience, technical skill, and analytical expertise needed on a performance audit team. Issues in resourcing include:

- relevant training

- specialized work experience

- specific technical skills

- interactive audit/management teams.

Some of the key skills needed for performance auditing include:

- comprehensive audit training

- a thorough knowledge of the industry

- understanding of management as a specific discipline

- internal audit training

- financial audit training and attestation standards knowledge

- effectiveness in communication

- an appreciation for multiple methods of analyzing data.

Thus, resourcing requires the performance audit manager to evaluate multiple facets of potential audit team members to achieve a balance which will be both cost effective and supply the necessary human resources to the performance audit engagement.

Referencing

Referencing is not a part of the audit itself; rather, it is the evaluation of the audit. Referencing assures that the summary and communication of the audit results is consistent with the audit findings and audit evidence. The referencing stage is that in which the audit is audited. The technique involves obtaining an independent person, who is not part of the audit team, to go back to the audit workpapers. In reviewing the audit workpapers, the auditors' auditor searches for fundamental themes in the audit evidence; these themes are inventoried and compared with the final product of the audit report. The purpose of referencing is for quality control: to insure that the audit report is supported by the audit evidence. This technique is particularly useful in the performance audit context because of the wide scope and comprehensiveness of the audit evidence.

VALUE FOR MONEY AUDITS AND SOCIAL ACCOUNTING DISCLOSURES

Surely the purpose of all accountability is to allow capital providers to monitor the uses of their funds. This is the most basic of justifications for performance auditing. Capital providers then have the power and knowledge to reallocate their capital in the private sector, or demand public sector reallocation from elected officials.

A recent Financial Accounting Standards Board deliberation resulted in a peculiar resolution. Because of the deleterious health effects of asbestos insulation in buildings, many building codes require asbestos removal or containment prior to occupancy. The accounting issue involved is whether to treat the asbestos removal or containment cost as an expense or as a capital item. Because expensing the cost has tax implications, differential accounting treatment of the item was being experienced in the real estate industry. For example, a potential seller who wished to minimize his gain on the sale of an asbestos-laden building may expense the cost; however, one who wished to show income on the sale would capitalize the same item and include it in the basis of the building. In addition, the seller could also achieve accounting flexibility by allowing the purchaser to book the asbestos removal or containment cost by having it done as a condition of the sale, but after the sale took place. Again, depending on the income/tax position of the buyer, it may have been booked as an expense, or recorded as an asset. Perusal of industry practice has found it recorded both ways. The costs are material, and this caused many corporations to solicit advice from the FASB regarding how to book the cost. In looking to the FASB to proscribe accounting practice for asbestos containment, the real estate industry was delighted to hear the FASB's decision: either booking an asset, or recording an expense, was acceptable. In October 1989, the Emerging Issues Task Force of the FASB forwarded a consensus decision which permits both expensing and capitalizing.

Aside from the theoretical problems of this illustration, social accounting issues are present. The theoretical problem is, at a minimum, to consider how the *removal of asbestos* is an asset, i.e., a future resource to the firm. While the presence of asbestos creates potential liabilities, its removal is a one-time action. Surely the building has no value with the asbestos present, since it cannot be occupied. However, it is not at all clear that the *absence of asbestos* is an asset, any more than the absence of toxic waste provides value to a parcel of land. If there is toxic waste, the land's value declines. But in the purchase of a "clean" site we would not attribute part of the land value to the fact that toxic waste was not present. In the same way, asbestos reduces value, but the absence of asbestos does not provide future value above the purchase price. The market does not value a prime commercial building that never had asbestos insulation differently from one in the same prime location in which the asbestos has been removed. In this way, it is theoretically deficient to call asbestos removal an asset with future earning potential. Rather than articulating the accounting treatment for the rather small number of accounting possibilities between buyers and sellers, the FASB chose to advocate choice.

This leads to social accounting issues. On the one hand, asbestos removal and containment procedures are more likely to be stringently enforced if the companies have wide flexibility to achieve management's financial reporting objectives, and thereby avoid insolvency. On the other hand, it is easier to "bury" the cost on financial statements given the flexibility that companies have been accorded by the FASB. This means less uniformity and comparability in financial statements, and capital may not flow to the most efficient sectors of the economy. This, in turn, leads to inefficient use of capital in the global sense, depriving legitimate individual and business opportunities from maximizing wealth.

Performance auditing provides at least a partial solution to the above dilemma. In reporting value-for-money, quite literally here, the building value would be the same, regardless of how financial accounting booked the transaction. The economic value of the building is its market value as determined by factors external to the accounting system, such as location, condition, size, and configuration. Performance accounting and auditing is able to handle the transaction by including qualitative and quantitative data external to the financial accounting system. The capital market providers receive benefits by knowledge and assurance provided by the performance audit report. The *financial audit* would reveal the cash flow involved in removing the asbestos. But this alone is not sufficient information for investors, regulators, creditors, or the public at large. The *compliance audit* would report on the extent to which the asbestos containment or removal has been successful in meeting building codes; this information is useful to regulators, employees working in the building, and creditors who have loans secured by the building. The *operational audit* would include control system evaluation; this system should ensure that future asbestos problems will be revealed, that this information will come to the attention of management, and that management has a plan or policy to solve the problem. The *management audit* would include evaluation of the information that management receives, its timeliness and relevancy, and would also assess management's responsiveness in dealing with the problem. The management audit, then, provides useful information to investors and the public that they have proactive systems in place to avoid problems or to handle problems systematically in the future.

In summary, no one portion of the performance audit assures the public that they can have confidence that management of the asbestos-laden building achieved economy (removing asbestos or containing at the lowest possible cost), efficiency (removing or containing asbestos quickly without releasing excess fibers into the environment, using and safeguarding appropriately trained personnel for the job, using up-to-date technology for long-term security, etc.), and effectiveness (solving the current asbestos problem to the satisfaction of involved constituencies, and maintaining systems to detect and avoid future problems). But the financial, compliance, operational, and management audits, when evaluated *as a whole*, allow auditors to provide assurance to investors, regulators, creditors, and the public, that the asbestos problem is in an "in control" state.

What is the effect of this reporting latitude, and how can performance auditing help? The financial audit would confirm that cash flows went out of the firm for asbestos removal, whether it was booked as an expense or a capital asset. The internal audit would confirm that cost and other controls were in place which fostered cost effectiveness. The management audit would reveal whether systems were in place to monitor asbestos in the air, so that management would be alerted to ineffective asbestos removal. But in combination, the performance audit would evaluate whether the asbestos removal was done at least cost, with a minimum of resources, was done within legal environmental standards of effectiveness, and that management would be alerted to future problems through an operational strategic system. In a performance context, the expensing versus capitalizing of the cost is not significant as it is in the differential financial statements. Rather, the emphasis is on whether there was value obtained for the expenditure.

Finally, better and more comprehensive reporting results from comprehensive auditing. Performance auditing fulfills the function of providing confidence that the major operations and decision-making functions within an organization are "in control." The reporting of "out of control" systems in the organization, provides incentives to management to bring "out of control" sections or processes back into control, or risk losing their jobs or foregoing inflows of capital to the firm or the public entity.

Accountability to constituents fosters good management. Good management, in turn, positively influences the allocation of goods and services to economical, efficient, and effective enterprises and public offices. Surely there is no more valuable role any manager or auditor can play in the global marketplace.

Selected Bibliography

American Institute of Certified Public Accountants. Committee on Governmental Accounting and Auditing. *Industry Audit Guide on Audits of State and Local Governments*. Third edition. New York: AICPA. 1981.

American Institute of Certified Public Accountants. SEC Practice Section, Public Oversight Board. *In the Public Interest: Issues Confronting the Accounting Profession*. New York: AICPA. 1993.

Association of Certified Fraud Examiners. *The White Paper* 7:2 (April-May 1993): 25.

Auditing Concepts Committee. "Report of the Committee on Basic Auditing Concepts." *The Accounting Review* 47 (Supplement 1972): 18.

Auditor General of Canada. *Audit Guide; Auditing of Efficiency*. Ottawa: Auditor General of Canada. January 1981.

Auditor General of Canada. *Audit Guide; Auditing of Procedures for Effectiveness*. Ottawa: Auditor General of Canada. August 1981.

Auditor General of Canada. *Auditing for Effectiveness*. Ottawa: Auditor General of Canada. August 1981.

Belkaoui, A. *Socio-economic Accounting*. Westport, CT: Greenwood Press. 1984.

Blessing, Linda J. "New Opportunities: A CPA's Primer on Performance Auditing." *Journal of Accountancy* (May 1991): 58–68.

Boland, Brian. "Performance Auditing Techniques and Reporting." *Australian Accountant* (May 1987): 57–60.

Bradshaw, J. "The Concept of Need." *New Society* 30 (1972).

Canadian Comprehensive Auditing Foundation. *Comprehensive Auditing: Concepts, Components, and Characteristics*. Ottawa: Canadian Comprehensive Auditing Foundation. 1983.

Canadian Institute of Chartered Accountants. Public Sector Accounting and Auditing Committee. *Public Sector Auditing Statement #4, Value-for-Money Auditing Standards*. March 1988.

Canadian Institute of Chartered Accountants. Public Sector Accounting and Auditing Committee. *Public Sector Auditing Guideline 1: Planning Value-for-Money Audits*. Ottawa, Canada: Canadian Institute of Chartered Accountants. March 1990.

Carson, Paul and Kerry D. Carson. "Deming Versus Traditional Management Theorists on

Goal Setting: Can Both Be Right?" *Business Horizons* 3:5 (September-October 1993): 79–84.

Committee on Nonprofit Entities' Performance Measures, American Accounting Association Government and Nonprofit Section. *Measuring the Performance of Nonprofit Organizations: The State of the Art.* Sarasota, FL: American Accounting Association. 1989.

Conference Board. *Report Number 974: Employee Buy-in to Total Quality.* New York: The Conference Board. 1991.

Cutt, James. *Comprehensive Auditing in Canada: Theory and Practice.* New York: Praeger. 1988.

Duquette, Dennis and Alexis M. Stowe. "A Performance Measurement Model for the Office of the Inspector General." *Government Accountants Journal* (Summer 1993): 27–49.

Durant, Robert F. and Laura A. Wilson. "Public Management, TQM, and Quality Improvement: Toward a Contingency Strategy." *American Review of Public Administration* 23:3 (September 1993): 215–45.

Elliott, Robert K. "The Future of Audits: The Power of Information Technology is Threatening the Audit Function." *Journal of Accountancy* (September 1994): 74–82.

Enthoven, Adolph. "International Management Accounting: Its Scope and Standards." *The International Journal of Accounting, Education, and Research* 17:2 (Spring 1982): 59–74.

Feigenbaum, Armand. "Linking Quality Processes to International Leadership." *Making Total Quality Happen: Conference Board Research Report No. 937.* Frank Caropreso, ed. New York: Conference Board. 1990.

Financial Accounting Standards Board. *EITF Consensus 93-5. Accounting for Environmental Liabilities.* Stamford, CT: FASB. 1993.

Frank, W. G. "An Empirical Analysis of International Accounting Principles." *Journal of Accounting Research* 17:1 (Autumn 1979): 369–605.

Glynn, John J. *Value for Money Auditing in the Public Sector. Research Studies in Accounting.* London: Prentice Hall International. 1985.

Grant, Robert M., Rami Shani, and R. Krishnan. "TQM's Challenge to Management Theory and Practice." *Sloan Management Review* 35:2 (Winter 1994): 25–35.

Gross, Martin L. *The Government Racket: Washington Waste From A to Z.* New York: Bantam Books. 1993.

Hegarty, John. "GATT: A Chance to Take the Lead." *Accountancy* 113:1206 (February 1994): 72–73.

Hegarty, John, Lane A. Daley and Gerhard G. Mueller. "Accounting in the Arena of World Politics: Crosscurrents of International Standard-Setting Activities." *Global Accounting Perspectives.* Jagdish Sheth and Abdolreza Eshghi, eds. Cincinnati: Southwestern Publishing Co. 1989.

Hendricks, M. "Service Delivery Assessment: Qualitative Evaluations at the Cabinet Level." *New Directions for Program Evaluation: Federal Efforts to Develop New Evaluation Methods.* N. Smith, ed. San Francisco: Jossey-Bass. 1981.

Henley, Douglas, Clive Holtham, Andrew Likierman, and John Perrin. *Public Sector Accounting and Financial Control.* Berkshire, England: The Chartered Institute of Public Finance and Accountancy/ Van Nostrand Reinhold (UK). 1983.

Herzlinger, Regina E. and Denise Nitterhouse. *Financial Accounting and Managerial Control for Nonprofit Organizations.* Cincinnati: South-Western Publishing Co. 1994.

Jackall, Robert. *Moral Mazes: The World of Corporate Managers.* London: Oxford University Press. 1988.

———. "Moral Mazes: Bureaucracy and Managerial Work." In *Ethics in Practice: Managing the Moral Corporation.* Kenneth R. Andrews, ed. Boston: Harvard Business

School Press. 1989.

Kaplan, Robert S. and David P. Norton. "The Balanced Scorecard—Measures that Drive Performance." *Harvard Business Review* (January-February 1992): 71–79.

Kelley, Thomas P. "The COSO Report: Challenge and Counterchallenge." *Journal of Accountancy* (February 1993): 10–18.

Kelly, Brian. *Adventures in Porkland: How Washington Wastes Your Money and Why They Won't Stop*. New York: Villard Books. 1993.

Kusserow, Richard P. "Program Inspections." *The Government Accountants Journal* (Spring 1984): 1–6.

Layfield Committee. *Local Government Finance: Report of the Committee of Enquiry*. CMNd. 6453, England: HMSO. 1976.

Lehman, C. R. *Accounting's Changing Role in Social Conflict*. New York: Markus Wiener, Inc. 1992.

Mandel, E. "In Defense of Socialist Planning." *New Left Review* 159 (1986).

Maskell, Brian. *Performance Measurement for World Class Manufacturing: A Model of American Companies*. Cambridge, MA: Productivity Press. 1991.

Mueller, Gerhard G., Helen Gernon, and Gary K. Meeks. *Accounting, An International Perspective*. Third edition. Burr Ridge, IL: Irwin. 1994.

Owen, David. *Green Reporting: Accountancy and the Challenge of the Nineties*. London: Chapman & Hall. 1992.

Parker, Lee. "Towards Value for Money Audit Policy." *Australian Accountant* (December 1986): 79–82.

Patton, James M. "Accountability and Governmental Financial Reporting. *Financial Accountability and Management* 8:3 (Autumn 1992): 165–80.

Percy-Smith, J. "Auditing Social Needs: An Alternative Means of Evaluating Policy." *Seminar on Social Audit*. 1990.

Persaud, Narayan and David R. DiSilvo. "Some Things About Surveys They Forgot to Teach Us in Social Science 301: The Performance Audit Perspective." *Government Accountants Journal* (Winter 1992): 37–48.

Pomeranz, F. *The Successful Audit: New Ways to Reduce Risk Exposure and Increase Efficiency*. Homewood, IL: Business One Irwin. 1992.

Radin, Beryl A. and Joseph N. Coffee. *Public Administration Quarterly* 17:1 (Spring 1993): 42–54.

SAB 92. *Accounting and Disclosures Relating to Loss Contingencies*. 1994.

Sheldon, D. R. and E. F. McNamara. *Value-for-Money Auditing in the Public Sector*. Altamonte Springs, FL: Institute of Internal Auditors Research Foundation. 1991.

Steele, Anthony. *Audit Risk and Audit Evidence: The Bayesian Approach to Statistical Auditing*. London: Academic Press Limited. 1992.

Sweeney, Paul. "Accounting: Making Sense of Chinese Books." *Global Finance* 7:4 (April 1993): 29–30.

Tracy, Richard C. "Performance Auditing Techniques and Reporting." *Australian Accountant* (May 1987): 57–60.

Treadway Commission. "An Integrated Framework for Internal Control." Washington, DC: National Commission on Fraudulent Financial Reporting. March 12, 1991.

"23 Years into EPA's Mandate, Public Protection Seen Lacking." *The Washington Post* May 24, 1993, A 17:24.

U.S. Comptroller General. *Training and Related Efforts Needed to Improve Financial Management in the Third World*. Washington, DC: U.S.G.P.O. 1979.

U.S. House of Representatives. Committee on Government Operations. *Managing the Federal Government: A Decade of Decline*. 1993.

Wooldridge, Blue. "Increasing the Productivity of Public-Sector Training." *Public Productivity Review* XII:2 (Winter 1988): 205–17.

Index

About the Author

D. R. SHELDON is a professor in the School of Business and Public Management, The George Washington University, Washington, D.C. She specializes in financial management, accountancy, and controllership, with other interests in regulatory issues in business. Among her various publications are "Value-for-Money Auditing in the Public Sector: Strategies for Accountability in the 1990s" (1991) and "Research in Governmental Financial Management" (1989).